The Past in Question

Series Editor: J.F. Aylett

The Viking Age

Alan Farmer

Hodder & Stoughton
LONDON SYDNEY AUCKLAND TORONTO

Acknowledgements

The author and publishers thank the following for permission to reproduce copyright illustrations:

Reproduced by Courtesy of the Trustees of the British Museum, p 17; English Heritage, p 5; Michael Holford Photographs, p 45 both; Jorvik Viking Centre, York Archaeological Trust, p 34, 35 all; The Mansell Collection, p 41; National Museum Copenhagen, Denmark, p 39; National Museum of Iceland/Gisli Gestsson, p 37; Popperfoto, p 14; The Royal Commission on the Ancient & Historical Monuments of Scotland, p 23; The Society of Antiquaries of London, p 19; Statens Historiska Museer Stockholm, p 11 bottom; University Museum of National Antiquities, Oslo, Norway/L Smestad, p 6 both, p 9 left, p 11 top; Jac Brun, p 13 bottom, p 15; Erns Schwitters, p 16 bottom; Werner Forman Archive, p 9 right.

Hodder & Stoughton

British Library Cataloguing in Publication Data

Farmer, Alan
The Viking age. – (The past in question).
1. Vikings
I. Title II. Series
948.022

ISBN 0 340 52306 9

First published 1990

Typeset by Keyset Composition, Colchester.
Printed in Great Britain for the educational publishing division of Hodder and Stoughton Ltd, Mill Road, Dunton Green, Sevenoaks, Kent by St Edmundsbury Press Ltd, Bury St Edmunds.

Contents

1 The Start of the Viking Age

In 789 AD three foreign ships landed at a beach in Dorset. Beaduheard, a servant of the King of Wessex, rode down to the sea to try to find out where the ships were from, what their purpose was, and who commanded them.

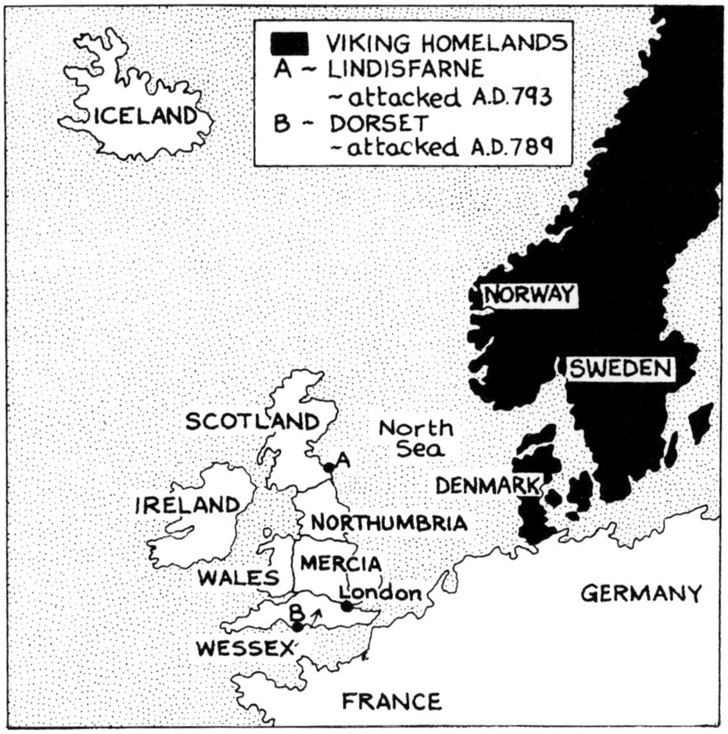

The Viking homelands.

Unfortunately for Beaduheard, the men in the three ships were far from friendly. He and the men who rode with him were killed.

In June 793 AD, **pagans** from the northern regions attacked Lindisfarne, a famous abbey, on Holy Island off the coast of Northumbria. They looted the church and killed or **enslaved** many of the monks. This attack shocked Christians throughout western Europe. 'Never before', wrote one monk, 'has such terror come to Britain.'

Today the men who killed Beaduheard and the warriors who attacked Lindisfarne are usually known as the Vikings. The Viking attacks on England in 789 and 793 AD were to be the first of many. For much of the 9th, 10th and 11th centuries, Viking warriors **terrorised** not just England but also Ireland, Scotland, France, the Netherlands and Germany.

The Vikings attack Lindisfarne.

The Vikings came from Denmark, Norway and Sweden. These countries today make up Scandinavia. But few people in Europe at this time had much idea about where the Vikings came from, or what exactly to call them.

In England the Vikings were usually called 'Danes', even when they came from what is today Norway or Sweden. In Ireland they were called 'Gaill' – or foreigners. French writers called them 'Northmen'. In eastern Europe they were called 'Varangians' or 'Rus'. Strangely enough, no one in the 9th and 10th centuries actually called them Vikings!

The exact meaning of the word Viking is a mystery, but probably comes from the Norse word 'vik' which means a bay or creek. To go 'a-Viking' meant sailing across the sea to gain riches and honour.

From the 9th to the 11th century, many **Scandinavians** – Norwegians, Danes and Swedes – were to go 'a-Viking'. They had such an effect on the whole of Europe that this period is often known as the 'Viking Age'.

A *From the* Anglo-Saxon Chronicle, *written in England in the Viking Age.*

While the most Christian King Brihtric was reigning over Wessex . . . a small fleet of Danes numbering three fast ships came unexpectedly to the coast; and this was their first coming.

Hearing of this the King's official, then staying at the town of Dorchester, leapt on his horse with a small bodyguard and galloped to the port, thinking they were merchants, rather than enemies; and . . . he ordered them to be taken to the royal residence. But he and his men were promptly killed by them. The name of the official was Beaduheard.

B *This picture, carved on a stone, was found at Lindisfarne. It is over 1000 years old.*

C *Simeon of Durham, a monk, wrote this in the 12th century.*

In the same year [793 AD] the pagans from the northern regions came with a fleet of ships to Britain like stinging hornets, and spreading on all sides like fearful wolves, robbed, tore and slaughtered not only beasts of burden, sheep and oxen, but priests . . . and companies of monks and nuns. And they came to the church of Lindisfarne, and laid everything waste . . .

They trampled the holy places with foul steps, dug up the altars and seized all the treasures of the holy church. They killed some of the monks and took some away in chains.

D *Alcuin, a famous Northumbrian priest, wrote this letter in 793 AD.*

For nearly 350 years we and our ancestors have lived in this lovely land. Never before has such a terror come to Britain as this that we have suffered from a **heathen** race. Nor was it thought possible that such an invasion could come from the sea. Behold the church of St Cuthbert, spattered with the blood of priests of God, robbed of all its **ornaments**.

Activities

1 Copy out and complete this paragraph.

The Vikings came from D________, N________, and S________. In 789 AD a group of Vikings landed near D________ in England and killed a servant of B________, King of Wessex. In 793 AD Viking raiders destroyed the church at L________ on H________ Island. In the 9th century Viking warriors attacked England, S________, I________, and F________.

2 a) Read source A. Why did Beaduheard ride out to meet the Danes?
b) Why do you think the Danes killed Beaduheard and his men?

3 a) Look at source B. Describe what you think the picture shows.
b) Why do you think some historians think the figures are Vikings?

4 a) Read sources C and D. Do you think the writers liked or disliked the Vikings? Why do you think this was?
b) Which of the two sources do you think is the most reliable and why?

5 Design a wanted poster, offering a reward and giving some information about either the murder of Beaduheard in 789 AD or the attack on Lindisfarne in 793 AD.

2 How Do We Know About the Vikings?

Historians today have different views about the Vikings. Some think they were savage killers, robbers and pirates. Others, however, think that their crimes have been exaggerated. They see them instead as great traders, explorers, craftsmen and artists.

The reason why there are different views is because historians interpret the surviving sources in different ways.

Unfortunately not many written sources from the Viking Age have survived. Few people at the time could read and write.

The main written sources are Chronicles. These are year-by-year accounts of important events, rather like diaries. They were kept in several countries that were attacked by the Vikings, including England, Ireland and France. The Vikings themselves have left no Chronicles.

The Chronicle writers were usually Christian monks. They hated and feared the Vikings, partly because the Vikings were not Christians, and also because they attacked churches and monasteries. So it could be that the Chronicles give us a very unfair view of the Vikings.

The best written sources which tell us what the Vikings thought are poems and **sagas**. These were first written down in the 12th and 13th centuries, many years after the real Viking Age was over. Some of the poems tell of events in everyday Viking life. Many of the sagas are about Viking heroes who had exciting adventures. Historians have to treat the sagas with care because they are rather like historical novels, part history and part fiction.

But historians do not rely just on written evidence. They can also use archaeological sources. These include coins, weapons, household goods, and the remains of houses and boats.

The early Vikings were not Christian. When they buried their dead they often put goods in the graves, hoping that this would help the dead on the way to the next world. Viking graves, therefore, provide archaeologists with a lot of evidence about the Vikings.

Recently a great deal of archaeological evidence about the Vikings has been discovered in York. If you go to the Jorvik Museum you can see some of the Viking discoveries. You can also see a modern reconstruction of what life in York may have been like in Viking times.

A *These carved objects, a wooden wagon and an animal's head, were found in a queen's grave at Oseberg in Norway. They were buried in the 9th century.*

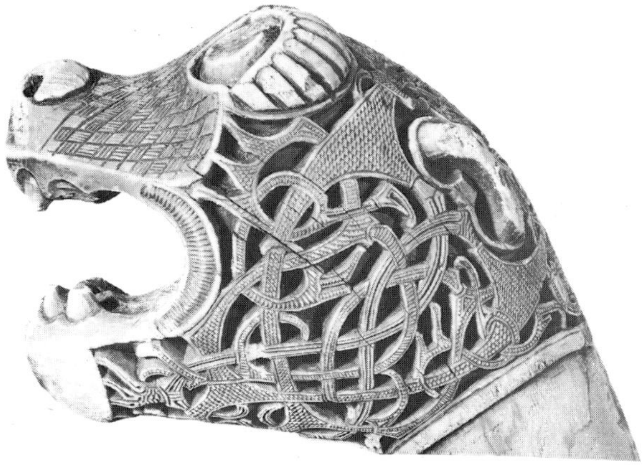

B *This is a diagram of a Viking grave discovered at Birka in Sweden. All the flesh, cloth and wood had rotted away. Only bone and metal were left.*

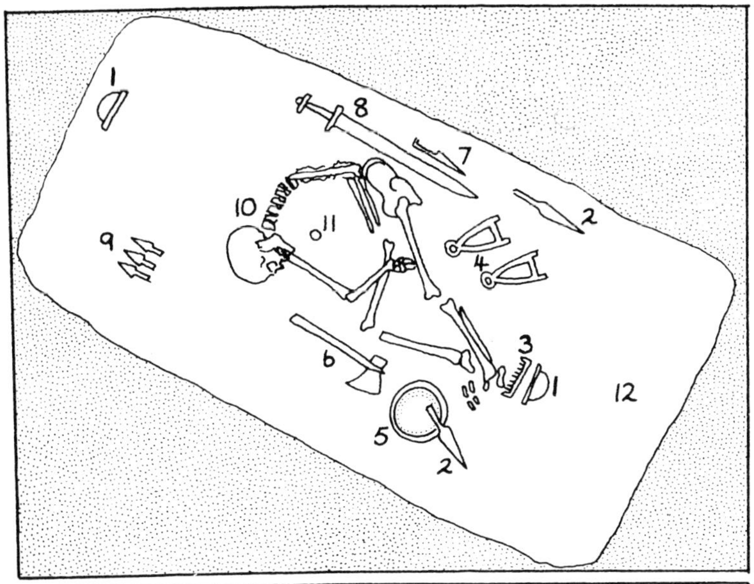

KEY
1. METAL BOSSES (CENTRES OF SHIELDS)
2. SPEARHEADS
3. COMB
4. STIRRUPS
5. BOWL
6. AXE
7. KNIFE
8. SWORD
9. ARROWHEADS
10. THE BODY
11. ARABIC COIN (MADE ABOUT A.D. 930)
12. REMAINS OF TWO HORSES

C *An extract from the* Anglo-Saxon Chronicle. *This was started by King Alfred the Great of Wessex at the end of the 9th century.*

869 . . . In this year the Viking army went across Mercia into East Anglia, and took winter quarters at Thetford; and the same winter St Edmund the king fought against them, and the Danes won the victory, and they slew the king and overran the entire kingdom, and destroyed all the monasteries to which they came. At the same time they came to the monastery at Peterborough and burned and demolished it, and slew the abbot and monks and all that they found there, reducing to nothing what had once been a very rich place.

D *An Icelandic poem called the* Havamal, *written in the 12th century, gives some useful tips about how to survive in Viking times.*

Look carefully round doorways before you walk in;
you never know when an enemy might be there.
Never part with your weapons when out in the fields;
you never know when you will need your spear.
Ale is not good for a man: the more he drinks the less control he has of his wits.

E *This is a famous story from the* Jomsvikings' Saga, *written in the 13th century. It is about a Viking called Thorkel Lara. After a battle he lined up the prisoners and cut off the heads of nine of them with his sword.*

The tenth prisoner was led forward. He was young and had long, silky yellow hair. Thorkel said, 'How do you like dying?' The man said, 'I have lived the best part of my life anyway – but I'm worried about getting blood on my hair. Get a good fighting man to hold it out of the way while you kill me.' A soldier came over and wound the hair round his hands. Thorkel raised his sword and brought it down as quickly as he could. When the young man heard it whistle in the air he threw himself backwards and the sword hit the man who was holding his hair. Both his arms were cut off at the elbows. The young man jumped up and said, 'What are these hands doing in my hair?'

Activities

1 a) Look at source A. Describe both objects.
b) What impressions do you get of the Vikings from these objects?

2 a) Look at source B. Which objects might provide clues as to when the person was buried?
b) What sort of person (male/female? rich/poor?) do you think was buried in the grave? Explain your answer.

3 a) Read source C. What impression do you get of the Vikings from this source?
b) You are a Viking chronicler. Write down your version of the events of 869 AD.

4 a) Read sources D and E. If you were a detective, what conclusions might you come to about life in Viking times from these sources?
b) Write what you think is a good ending for source E.

5 Work in groups. From the evidence in the sources, make a list of reasons why the Vikings might be thought to be **civilised**. Make another list of reasons why the Vikings might be thought to be uncivilised. Explain your lists to the other groups.

3 Why Did the Vikings Go a-Viking?

People from Scandinavia had traded with most parts of Europe from Roman times onwards. Even so, only a few Scandinavians had sailed far overseas before 800 AD. In the 9th, 10th and 11th centuries more and more Scandinavians left their homelands and sailed to many different parts of the world. Why did this happen?

One of the main reasons was that there were too many people in Scandinavia and not enough fertile land to go round. Many Vikings sailed overseas hoping to find land on which to settle or win wealth with which to buy land.

By the start of the 9th century, some Vikings were aware that many of their neighbours were weak. There was no strong state in eastern Europe. In western Europe, Charlemagne (768–814 AD) had built up a great empire which included most of present-day France, Belgium, Germany and Italy. After Charlemagne's death, however, his empire began to break up. Britain was divided into many small kingdoms which often fought amongst themselves.

Many areas of western Europe were richer than Scandinavia. There were several wealthy towns like London and Paris. There were also many rich churches and monasteries.

Vikings who sailed overseas often returned with news of easy pickings to be gained by those brave enough to win them. Some Vikings longed to do great deeds and win fame – and wealth.

Some Vikings seem to have gone sailing in the summer months because there was little to do on their farms. A trading or raiding voyage was a good way of growing rich.

Others seem to have gone a-Viking because they had committed crimes or been driven off their lands by stronger neighbours.

Europe in the Viking Age.

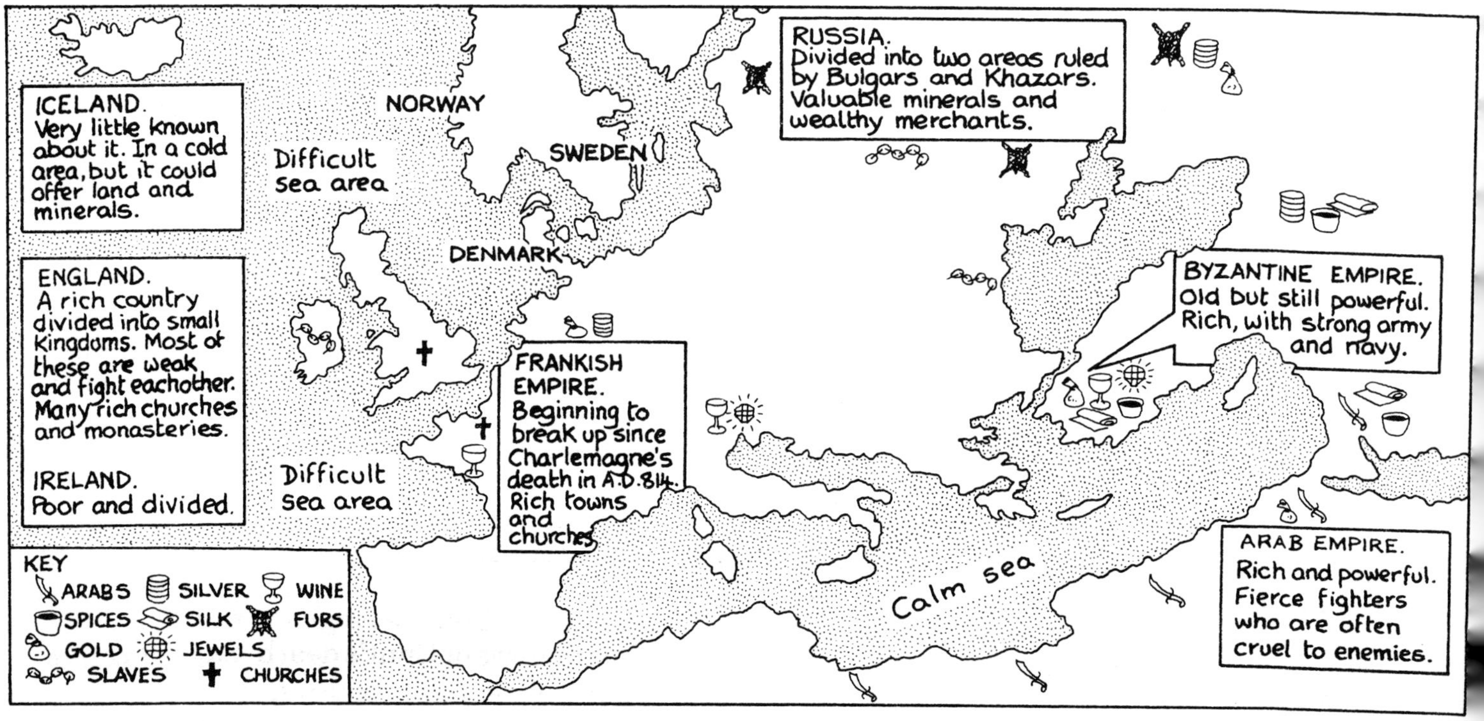

Perhaps the main reason why the Scandinavians went a-Viking from the late 8th century onwards is because they had the means to do so. Their shipbuilding methods improved. The Vikings were able to sail overseas to trade, raid, and discover new lands.

A *A photograph of the Gokstad ship, buried in Norway in the 10th century. It is thought to be a typical Viking longship.*

B *This is part of* Egil's Saga, *written in Iceland in the 13th century.*

In the summer they went on Viking voyages, conquered land and divided the spoils among themselves. In the winter they stayed at home with their fathers. In those days it was easy to gain riches and honour.

C *This was written by Adam of Bremen, a German, who lived at the end of the 11th century.*

Denmark consists almost entirely of islands. The poor soil is hardly farmed at all, and large towns only exist where fiords [deep inlets] cut into the land . . . Norway is the harshest of all countries because of its rugged mountains and extreme cold . . . Forced by the poverty of their homeland [the Norwegians] venture abroad to bring back from their raids the goods which other countries so plentifully produce. But much of Sweden is fertile and the land is rich in fruit and honey.

D *A typical picture of Norway today.*

Activities

1 a) Look at source D. Why would such land not have been good for farming?
b) Why do you think the sea was so important to the Norwegians who lived in areas such as this?
c) In what way does this source agree with source C?

2 Look at source A. How many men do you think might fit into the Gokstad ship? Explain how you decided.

3 According to source C, which Scandinavian people were probably the least likely to go a-Viking? Explain your answer.

4 Look at the map. If you were a Viking which area do you think would be the best to sail to if you wanted to (a) trade, (b) raid, (c) settle? Explain the reasons for your choices.

5 In groups, examine all the sources. Decide which you think were the five most important reasons why the Vikings went a-Viking. Put the reasons in a top-five order. Choose someone to explain your list to the rest of the class.

4 Viking Ships

For 300 years the Vikings were the best shipbuilders in Europe. They made ships that were good enough to sail to America.

We know something about Viking ships from written sources, especially the sagas. A few pictures, carved on wood or engraved on stone or on coins, have also survived. Yet the best evidence comes from the remains of Viking ships which have been discovered in the last 120 years. From all these sources it is clear that Viking ships were built in many shapes and sizes.

Probably the most famous type of Viking ship is the warship or 'longship'. These were shallow, fast boats used for raiding. In 1880 an amazingly well-preserved longship was found buried at Gokstad in Norway. It was buried some time between 850 and 900 AD.

The Gokstad ship could hold a crew of at least 34 men and possibly twice that number if necessary. When fully laden, it could sail in water about a metre deep.

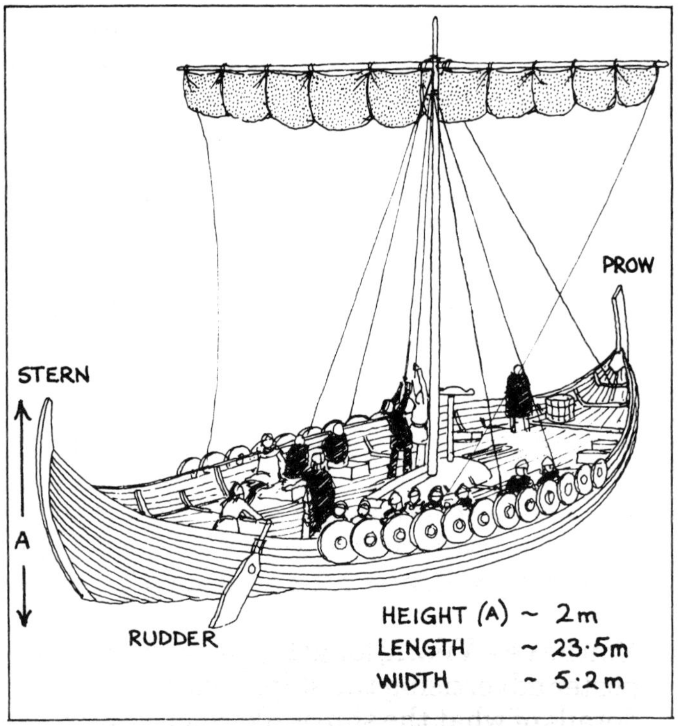

The Gokstad longship.

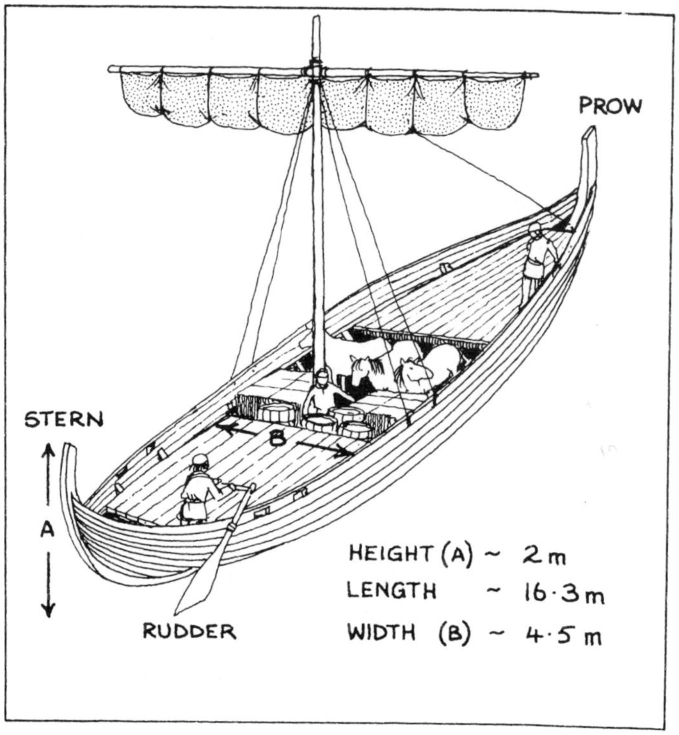

The Roskilde knorr.

The ship had a cloth sail, a single yard-arm, and a single mast that could easily be raised or lowered. It also had 16 oars, worked through holes, on either side.

Viking longships were able to move quickly in all kinds of weather. They could also land on sloping beaches and sail up shallow rivers. As they were made with thin planking, they could even be dragged overland.

The Vikings also built ocean-going ships which are usually known as **knorrs.** These were slower and tubbier than longships but sturdier and more seaworthy. Knorrs were mainly used by merchants or by Vikings who were hoping to settle in new lands overseas.

In 1962 an 11th-century knorr was recovered from under the sea at Roskilde Fiord in Denmark. This ship had higher sides than the Gokstad ship and could hold more cargo. It was not as easy to row but probably needed only a six- to twelve-man crew.

A *A photograph of the* **excavation** *of the Gokstad ship in 1880. (It took Norwegian archaeologists 60 years to reconstruct the ship.)*

B *Part of* King Harald's Saga, *written in Iceland in the 13th century.*

That winter King Harald had a ship built at Eyrar. It was much broader than normal warships . . . and most carefully built in every detail. Its prow had a dragon's head, and the stern had a dragon's tail, and the bows were decorated with gold. It had 35 pairs of rowing benches, with plenty of space between each; it was indeed a magnificent vessel. The King had all the fittings of the ship made with the utmost care, the sails and rigging as well as the anchor and ropes.

C *From a sculptured stone at Stenkyrka, Gotland in Sweden. (This was carved during the Viking Age.)*

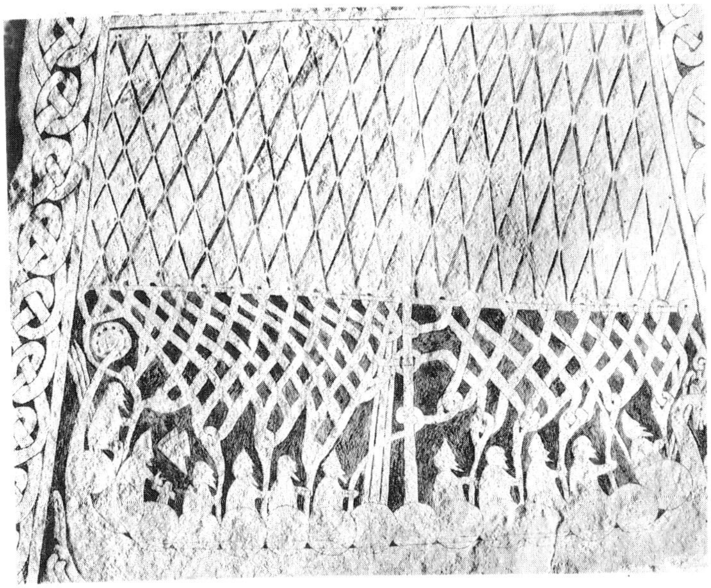

D *Dr McGrail, a 20th-century expert on Viking ships, wrote this in 1982.*

In 1893, 'Viking', a Norwegian **replica** of the Gokstad ship, under the command of Captain Magnus Andersen, sailed from Bergen to Newfoundland [an island off Canada] in 28 days. This voyage demonstrated the seaworthiness [of the ship] . . . The vessel successfully endured several stormy days and proved reasonably watertight. Viking ships were designed to be supple and to 'ride the punch' of the sea, rather than be rigid and battle against it . . . Leakage at the seams and through fastenings must always have been a problem, however, and bailing out a constant task . . . Captain Andersen was also favourably impressed by the side rudder which . . . he found easy to use even in heavy seas.

Activities

1 a) Draw up a table listing the main differences between the Gokstad longship and the Roskilde knorr. The following headings might help: length, width, depth, speed, sources of power, size of crew, purpose.
b) In what ways were the longship and the knorr similar?
c) Look at Source C. Do you think this is a picture of a knorr or a longship? Give reasons for your answer.

2 a) Look at Source A. Can you think of any reasons why the Gokstad ship might have been buried on land?
b) Why might we have to be careful in deciding what Viking ships were like from simply examining the Gokstad ship?

3 Read source B. In what ways was King Harald's ship different to the Gokstad ship?

4 a) Read source D. In what ways did the replica longship prove itself to be a good ship?
b) What problems did the ship have?

5 You have a Viking longship for sale. Draw a poster advertising the ship. Include some details of what the ship is like such as size, shape and any extras. Give your ship a name.

5 Viking Shipbuilding

Viking longships were built by a team of men. These men were led by a master boatbuilder or shipwright. Shipwrights were very skilled craftsmen. They did not work to written plans, but designed each ship as they went along.

At least twelve trees were needed to build an ordinary longship. The best ships were made almost completely of oak. But so many ships were built that oak became scarce. Pine, ash, beech, alder and willow were also used.

The most important and difficult thing was to find a single oak tree with a tall, straight trunk. This was needed for the keel. The keel was the backbone of the longship. Some trees would be cut into planks. This was done rather like slicing a cake. A wide tree gave 32 thin planks.

The shipwright would spend a lot of time working on the keel, prow and stern. These parts would take a battering from the sea and had to be joined together correctly.

Wood was not the only material used in shipbuilding. Iron was used for nails. Both whale and seal skin were used for ropes. Women had the long, hard job of weaving cloth to make sails.

The making of a Viking longship.

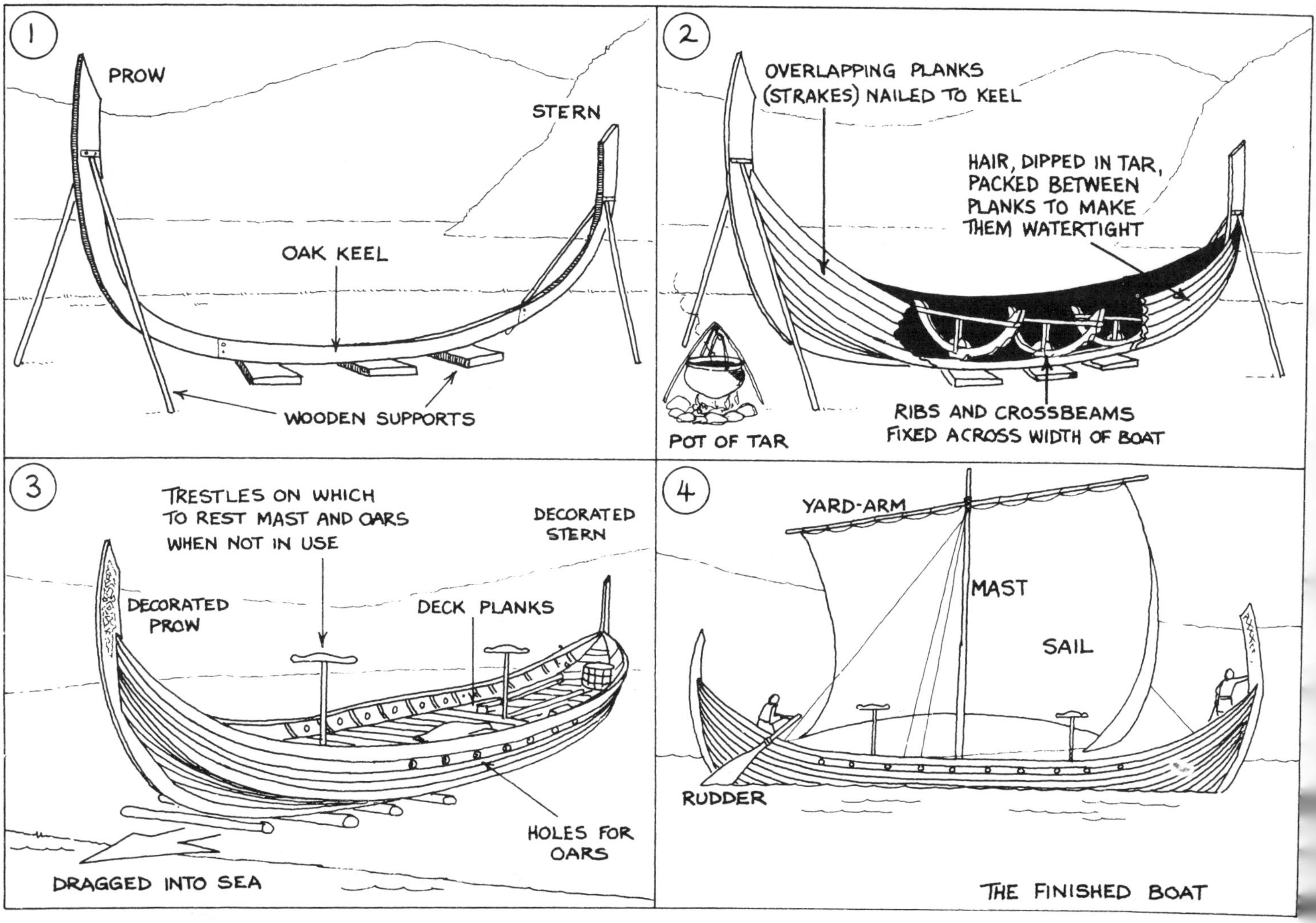

A *An artist's impression of a Viking ship under construction.*

B *The stern of the Oseberg ship. This ship was found in 1903 near Oslo. It once belonged to a Viking queen.*

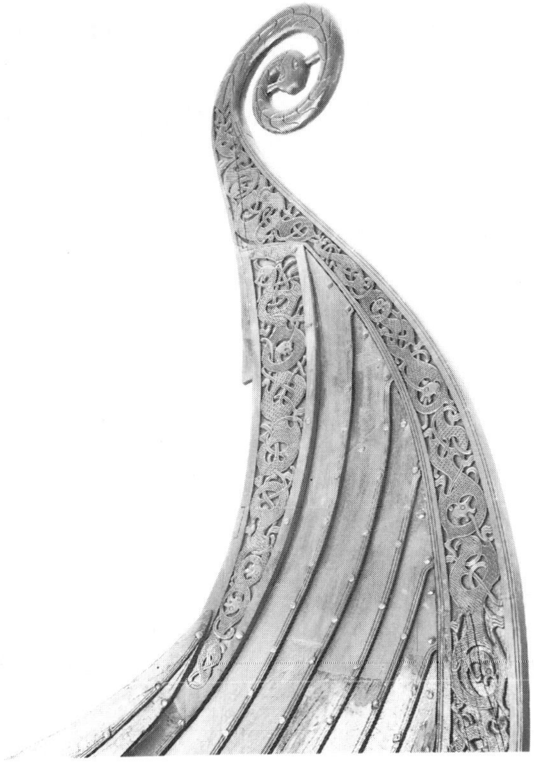

C *Types of tools used by craftsmen in Viking times.*

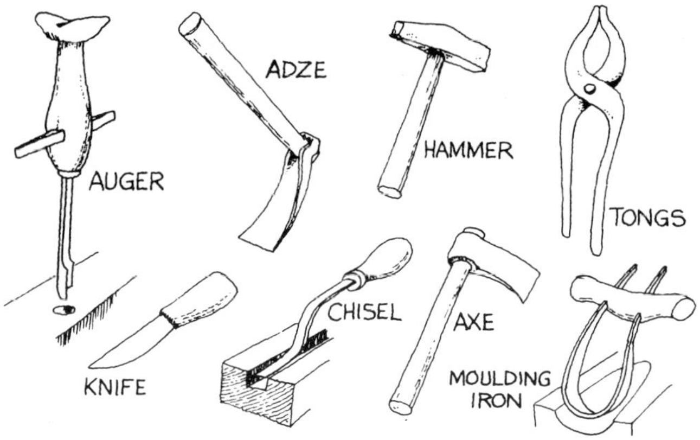

D *An Icelandic poet tells how a famous ship was built for King Olaf of Norway in the 10th century.*

King Olaf . . . had a great ship built . . . larger than any ship in the country . . . The keel was 36 metres long. Thornberg Skafhogg was in charge of making the bows and stern . . . but many others were involved. Some chopped down trees, some shaped them, some made nails, some carried timber . . . The ship was made of stout timber and had long, broad and high sides. While they were putting on the planks, Thornberg had to go home to his farm on urgent business . . . The ship was planked up on both sides when he came back . . . The King called the ship the Long Serpent . . . The Long Serpent had 34 benches for rowers. The bows and stern were covered with beaten gold.

Activities

1 Place the following events in order.

Putting in the ribs of the ship
Launching the ship
Making the keel
Adding the prow and stern
Putting on the strakes

2 a) Look at sources A and C. Describe what the men are doing in source A.
b) Which important wood-working tools do Viking shipbuilders not seem to have used?

3 Look at source B. What does this source show of Viking craftsmanship?

4 Read source D. Imagine you are Thornberg Skafhogg, the Viking shipwright. Describe how you made the 'Long Serpent'.

6 Life at Sea

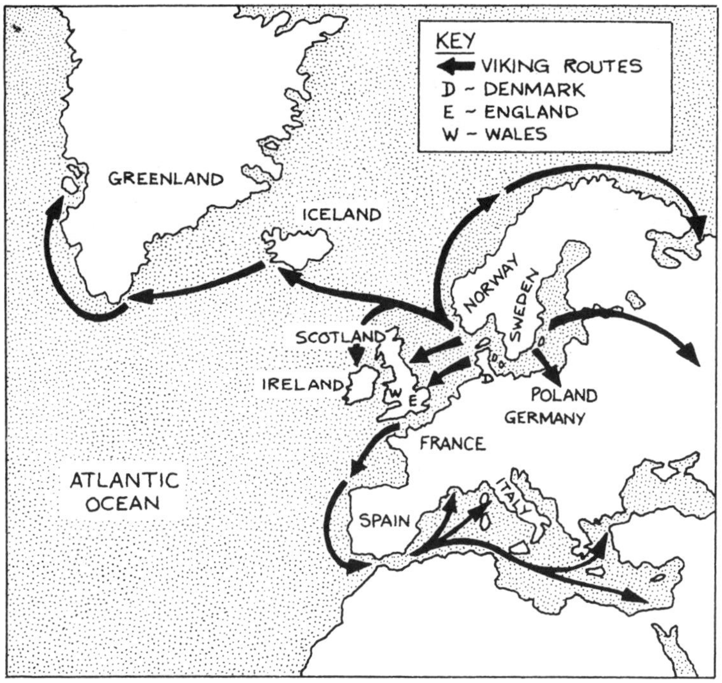

Places the Vikings visited.

Vikings went to sea for a variety of reasons – to fish, trade, raid, explore or to settle on new land. The sailing season was usually between April and October.

Travelling across the North Sea or the North Atlantic Ocean in a small ship, even in summer, must have been both uncomfortable and dangerous. There was little shelter in a Viking ship from the sea or the weather. Viking sailors must have spent many hours at sea bailing out water.

Vikings would hope to sail as much as possible. Sometimes, however, they would have to row. Unlike the Romans, the Vikings did not use slaves to work the oars. In most longships the rowers would sit close together on chests in which they kept their personal belongings.

The **helmsman** was the most important man on board most Viking ships. He was usually the captain and owner of the ship. A paddle, fixed at the stern on the starboard (right-hand) side, was used for steering.

Whenever possible, helmsmen steered close to land. Vikings liked to berth their ships and land at night. That way they could cook a hot meal and sleep in some comfort.

We do not know how the Vikings were able to find their way across open seas. Perhaps they had some simple **navigational instruments**. But so far none has been found and none is mentioned in written sources. It is likely, therefore, that the Vikings had to make do with the sun and stars, the experience of previous voyages, the sightings of birds and driftwood, and the 'feel' of the sea.

Battles at sea seem to have been rare. Those that did occur were usually fought in shallow water. Sometimes the Vikings would tie ships together and use them as a fighting platform.

A *A replica of a Viking longship which sailed across the Atlantic in 1893.*

B *A photograph of the deck of the Gokstad ship (shown on the right).*

C *Part of* King Harald's Saga – *written in Iceland in the 13th century.*

One Saturday, King Harald
Hauled down the deck-tent,
And the women proudly
Watched the ship speed past.
The young sea-king was steering
His new ship down the Nid,
While battle-hungry warriors
Dipped oars into the water.
Men will quake with terror
Before the seventy sea-oars
Are given deserved rest
From the labours of the ocean.
Norwegian arms are driving
The iron-nailed dragon
Down the storm-tossed river
Like the eagle on the wing.

D *Dr Sean McGrail, a 20th-century historian, wrote this description in 1982.*

Seamen, merchants and passengers slept where best they could on the deck . . . covered with hides or possibly in two-man, skin sleeping-bags for extra warmth. Food was mainly dried, pickled, salted or possibly smoked fish or meat, with **unleavened bread**. For drink there would be water in skin bags and beer or sour milk in tubs.

E King Harald's Saga. *King Harald of Norway, who had spent the summer raiding Denmark, came across King Svein of Denmark, who had a much larger fleet.*

Both fleets now rowed as hard as they could. The Danish ships were faster under oars, and the Norwegian ships were waterlogged and heavily laden, so the distance between them steadily narrowed.

Harald, whose own dragon-prowed ship was bringing up the rear, realised that this would not do . . . He ordered his men to lighten their ships as much as possible and throw overboard the **malt**, flour and bacon, and also to break open the wine-casks. This helped for a while. Then Harald ordered the empty casks and barrels to be thrown overboard, and also the Danish prisoners they had taken that summer. When King Svein saw the prisoners floating about in the sea, he gave orders for them to be rescued; but so much time was lost doing this that the Norwegians got away.

Activities

1 Look at Sources A and B. What might the T-shaped poles on the ships have been used for?

2 Look at the map. Which of the four voyages listed below do you think would have been the easiest and the hardest for a Viking captain to have made? Give reasons for your answers. Sweden to Poland; Denmark to Spain; Norway to Greenland; Norway to Ireland.

3 a) Read source E. Why do you think King Harald's Norwegian ships were 'heavily laden' and 'waterlogged'?
b) Do you think King Harald was right to lighten his ships by throwing the prisoners overboard? Explain your answer.
c) Do you think King Svein was right to stop and rescue the prisoners? Again explain your answer.

4 Work in groups. Try to list ten items which a Viking sea captain might have taken on board ship to make his trip more pleasant and safer. (Sources D and E might help.) Choose someone from your group to explain your choice of items to the other groups.

5 Read source C. Describe what it might have been like for a Viking captain setting sail on a raiding voyage and also describe what it might have been like on the longship for the first 24 hours at sea.

7 Viking Warriors

A Viking chieftain. *A Viking spearman.*

For 300 years Viking warriors were feared throughout Europe. Yet most Vikings did not earn a living as full-time fighters. Nor were their weapons or tactics very different from those of other warriors at that time.

Viking chieftains usually fought with swords. These were difficult to make and expensive to buy. They were imported into Scandinavia from Germany and France.

A few Vikings preferred the battle-axe. Some warriors are said to have been able to behead a horse with a single axe blow. Only wealthy Vikings owned a mail shirt or **byrnie**. This was made up of hundreds of small rings of metal fastened together.

Most Vikings probably went into battle carrying just a spear and shield, with only a sleeveless leather jacket for protection.

Strangely, Vikings don't seem to have worn horned or winged helmets, as is often believed. No such helmets have yet been found. Instead most warriors wore metal caps, sometimes with nose guards. Viking chiefs' helmets were sometimes richly decorated and had eye and cheek guards.

The Vikings almost always fought on foot, although they often used horses to get them to the battlefield. In battle, warriors usually formed a shield wall around their chief and then either defended their ground or attacked the enemy. Most chiefs would have a bodyguard of warriors who were known as **housecarls**. If their chief was killed they were expected to die with him.

The most feared Viking warriors were the **berserkers**. They were famed for their great strength and mad courage. Sometimes they would strip off their byrnies and attack almost naked. Perhaps they took some form of drug to give them extra strength and courage.

Many Vikings believed that if they died bravely in battle, they would go to **Valhalla** where they would feast with their gods.

Viking warriors had such a good reputation that the **Byzantine Emperors** in Constantinople paid for the **Varangian Guard**, a famous Viking regiment, to fight for them.

A *Weapons found in a 10th-century Viking grave.*

B *A wood-carving from the Viking Age.*

C *Ibn Miskawaih, an Arab traveller, wrote this description of the Vikings in the 10th century.*

They do not know the meaning of the word defeat. They never turn their backs on their enemies but kill or are killed. A Viking fights with spear and shield. He wears a dagger and has a throwing spear.

D *'The Battle of Maldon', an Anglo-Saxon poem, describes a battle between Vikings and Anglo-Saxons, fought in 991. Brihtnoth was an Anglo-Saxon warrior.*

Brihtnoth ordered his men to form a shield wall and hold their ranks bravely against the Viking foe. The battle was now at hand . . .

They let the spears, hard as files, fly from their hands. Bows were busy, point pierced shield; fierce was the rush of battle, warriors fell on all sides . . .

Then Brihtnoth raised his spear, gripped his shield and stepped towards one of the Danes. The Viking was the quicker – he hurled his spear, wounding Brihtnoth. Brihtnoth broke the spear shaft on the edge of his shield and pulled the spear-head from his body. In fury he flung his own spear . . .

His aim was skilful. The spear split open the Dane's neck and killed him.

E *Thorolf, a Viking warrior, is described in* Egil's Saga, *written in the 13th century.*

He wore a very strong helmet on his head, and had a broad, stout shield and a sword he called Long, a fine big weapon. In his hand he held a spear whose shaft was eight feet long . . .

Thorolf now grew so berserk that he swung his shield onto his back and seized his spear in both hands. Then he ran forward, cutting and thrusting to both right and left. Men fell back on either hand, but there were many he killed. Thus he cleared a path forward to Earl Hring's standard. Nothing could now stop him; he killed the man carrying Hring's standard, and cut down the standard pole, then thrust with his spear at the earl's breast. It went through mailshirt and body so that it came out between his shoulders.

Activities

1 Complete the sentences.
a) A byrnie was. . .
b) A berserker was. . .
c) A housecarl was. . .

2 a) Look at source A. List the weapons that were found in the grave.
b) Do you think this was the grave of an ordinary Viking or a chieftain? Explain your answer.

3 Look at source B. Describe what you think is happening in the picture.

4 a) Read sources D and E. In what way do they agree about how warriors fought in the Viking Age?
b) Which account sounds the most likely to have really happened? Explain your answer.
c) Draw four pictures, in comic form, to show the events described in source D or E.

5 You are a Byzantine agent who has been to Scandinavia. Write a report for the Emperor in Constantinople describing what Viking warriors are like and whether you think it is worth paying for their services.

8 The Vikings Attack England

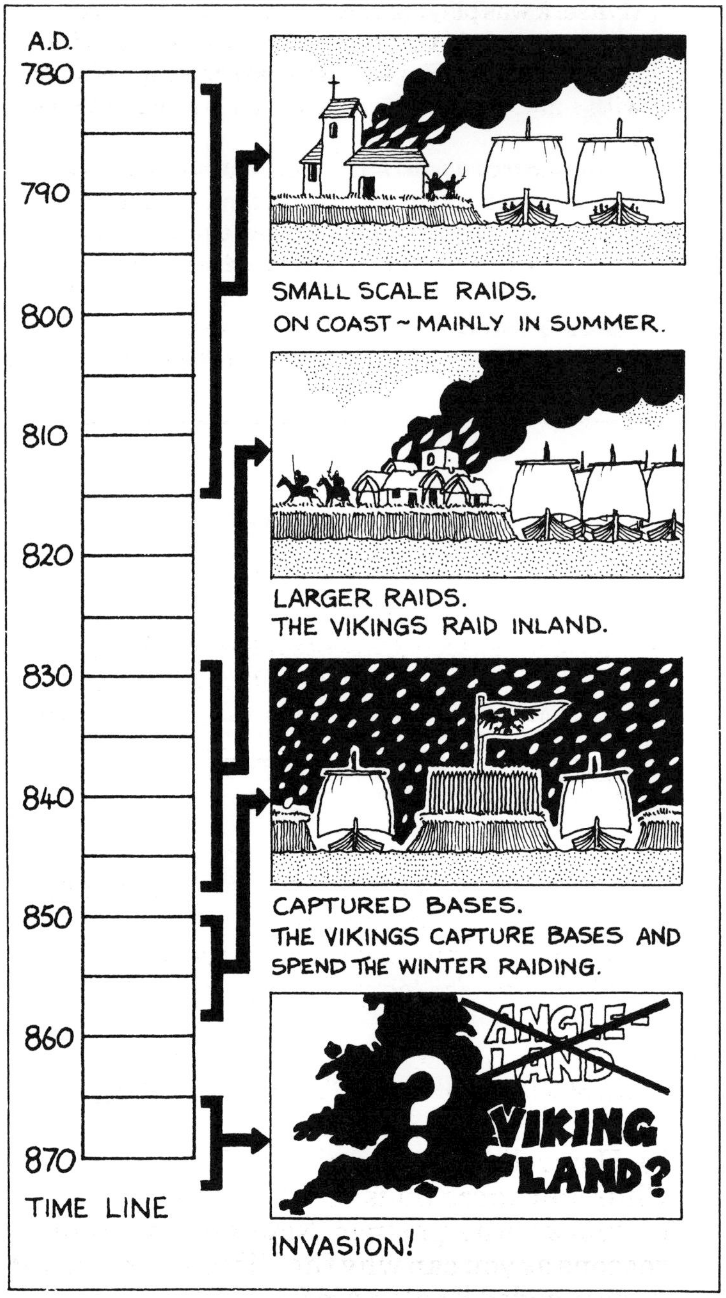

Viking attacks on England.

The first Viking attacks on England were mainly small-scale 'smash and grab' raids. A few Viking longships came without warning and plundered villages and monasteries near the coast. They attacked so quickly that it was hard to deal with them. By the time an army was ready, the Vikings had sailed away.

From 830 AD onwards there were more and more Viking attacks. Soon, Viking war bands were strong enough to take over small islands off the coast. They built forts, captured horses and raided deep into the heart of England.

A *A map showing the recorded Viking attacks on England from 789 to 865 AD.*

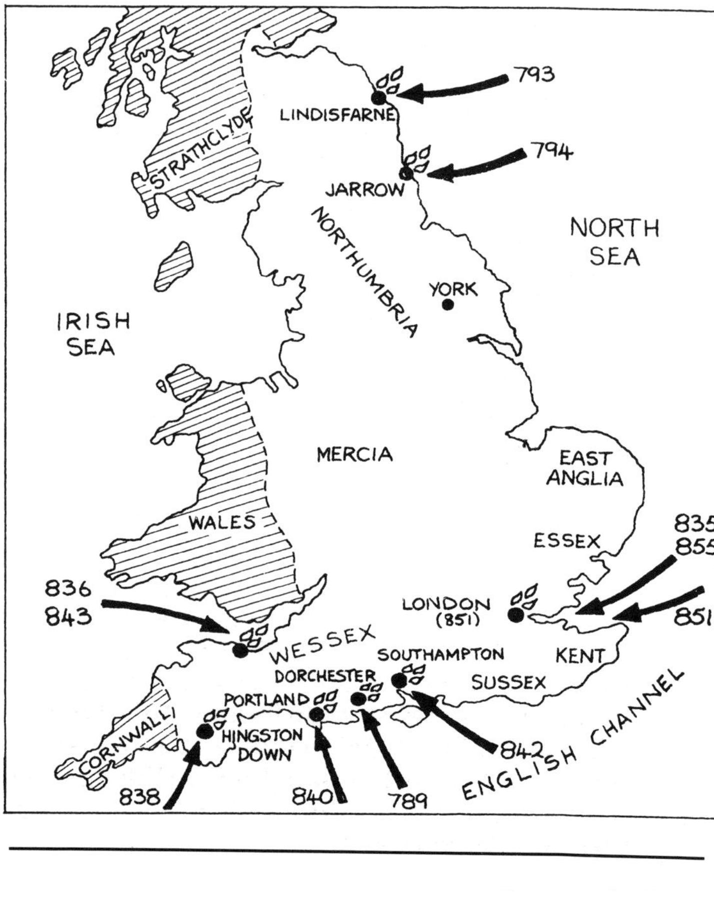

Sometimes they were defeated but there always seemed to be more Viking raiders.

In 865 AD a large Viking army, led by Ivar 'the Boneless', invaded East Anglia. It then attacked Northumbria, overran Mercia and captured York.

By 870 AD the only Anglo-Saxon kingdom which still held out against the Vikings was Wessex. Alfred, its new king, fought a series of desperate battles. In 871 AD he was forced to make peace. This gave Alfred time to strengthen his defences, but it also gave the Vikings time to increase their control over those parts of England which they had already conquered. It seemed possible that Angle-land might well become Viking-land!

B *A 10th-century drawing of the death of King Edmund of East Anglia.*

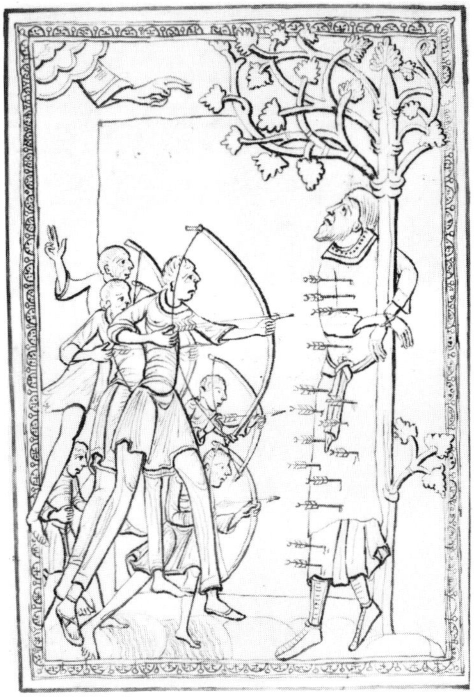

C *An extract from the* Anglo-Saxon Chronicle.

851. 350 ships came to the mouth of the Thames and stormed Canterbury and London, and put to flight Beorhtwulf, King of Mercia and his army, and then went south over Thames into Surrey; and King Aethelwulf and his son Aethelbald, with the West Saxon army, fought against them at Acleah, and there made the greatest **slaughter** of a Viking army that we have heard tell of up to this present day, and there won the victory.

D *This is from Sir Winston Churchill's* History of the English Speaking Peoples, *written in 1956.*

According to Scandinavian story, Ragnar Lodbrok [a Viking pirate] was captured by King Aelle of Northumbria, and cast into a snake-pit to die ... Ragnar had four sons and as he lay among the poisonous reptiles he uttered a great threat: 'The little pigs would grunt now if they knew how it fares with the old boar.'

The poets tell us how his sons received the news. Bjorn 'Ironside' gripped his spear shaft so hard that the print of his fingers remained stamped upon it. Hvitserk was playing chess, but he clenched his fingers so tightly that the blood started from under his nails. Sigurd 'Snake-eye' was trimming his nails with a knife, and kept on paring until he cut into the bone.

But the fourth son was the one who counted. Ivar 'the Boneless' demanded the precise details of his father's execution, and his face became red, blue and pale by turns and his skin appeared puffed up by anger ...

Ivar 'the Boneless' was ... the master-mind behind the Scandinavian invasion of England.

Activities

1 a) Look at source A. Make a list of all the kingdoms in England in the 9th century.
b) Why might the fact that there were several kingdoms in England have helped the Vikings?

2 a) Read source C. Why might King Aethelwulf have found the Vikings easier to beat than King Beorhtwulf?
b) Why might the chroniclers' account of the number of Viking ships not be correct?

3 a) Read source D. Why, according to Churchill, did Ivar 'the Boneless' lead the Viking invasion of England?
b) How reliable do you think Winston Churchill's account is? Give reasons.
c) Work with a partner. Note down as many reasons as you can why the Viking army might have invaded England in 865 AD.

4 Look at source B. Whose hand do you think is pointing from the sky and why?

9 The Kingdom of England

In 878 AD a Viking army, led by Guthrum, invaded Wessex. King Alfred was taken by surprise and fled to Athelney in the Somerset marshes. The Vikings overran much of Wessex but Alfred refused to surrender.

Instead he raised an army and defeated Guthrum at the battle of Edington. Guthrum was forced to make peace and promised not to attack Wessex again.

A few years later the two kings agreed to another **treaty**. This divided England into two. Alfred ruled the southern half. The northern half – **Danelaw** – remained under Viking control.

Alfred had not succeeded in driving the Vikings from England. But at least he and Wessex had survived. For this reason Alfred maybe deserves his nickname – 'the Great'.

Alfred's son, Edward the Elder, began to win back land from the Vikings. He was helped by Aethelflaed, his sister, who ruled Mercia until her death in 918 AD. By the time Edward died in 924 AD, all the Vikings south of the River Humber accepted him as their **overlord**.

Athelstan, Edward's son, was just as successful. He faced a new Viking threat. At the start of the 10th century, Vikings from Norway and Ireland began to settle in north-west England and soon linked up with the Danish Vikings in Yorkshire.

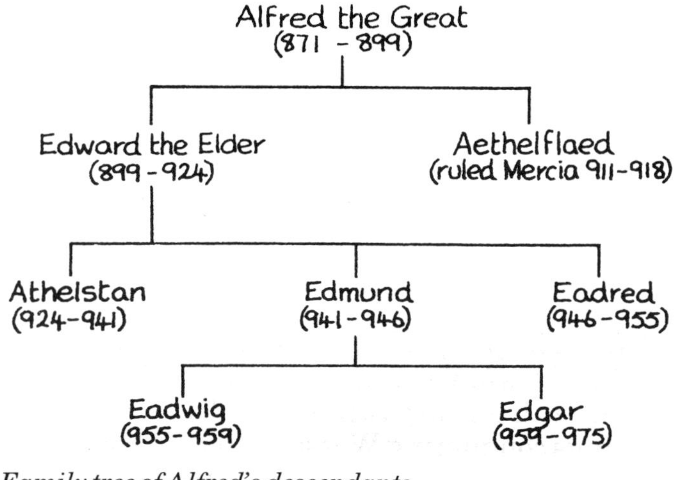

Family tree of Alfred's descendants.

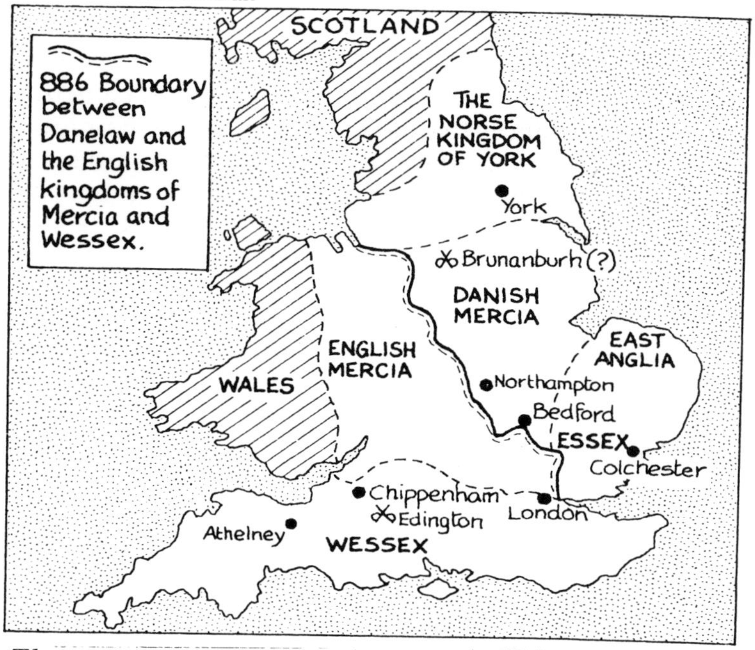

The reconquest of Danelaw.

Athelstan led his army north, drove out the Norse king of York, and forced all the Vikings in England and most of the kings in Scotland and Wales to accept him as overlord. He thus became the most powerful man to rule in Britain since Roman times. He is the first man who can claim to be king of all England.

In 937 AD a great alliance of Scots, Irish and Northumbrian Vikings joined forces against Athelstan. But he again marched north and defeated his enemies at Brunanburh. The exact site of this great battle is a mystery but it was probably fought near Sheffield.

Athelstan's brothers, Edmund and Eadred, continued to have trouble with the Viking north. But by 950 AD most Vikings had settled down on the land they had won. Many had English wives and do not seem to have worried too much about who ruled them, providing they were allowed to keep their land.

Edgar, Alfred's great-grandson, was accepted by Anglo-Saxons and Vikings as king of a united England. He ruled peacefully. The Viking threat to England seemed to be over.

A *This is from the* Anglo-Saxon Chronicle.

878. The Viking army went secretly in midwinter after Twelfth Night to Chippenham, and rode over Wessex, and occupied it, and drove a great part of the inhabitants overseas, and reduced the greater part of the rest, except Alfred the king; and he with a small company moved under difficulties through woods and into inaccessible places in marshes . . . King Alfred built a fort at Athelney, and . . . continued fighting against the Vikings. Then in the seventh week after Easter he rode to Ecgbert's Stone . . . and there came to meet him all the men of Somerset, Wiltshire and Hampshire . . . And he went to Edington; and there he fought against the entire Viking army, and put it to flight, and pursued it up to the fortifications, and laid siege there a fortnight; and then the Vikings gave him prisoners. They promised that they would leave Wessex, and also promised . . . that King Guthrum would became Christian. They kept their promises.

B *A 10th-century drawing showing a battle between Anglo-Saxon and Viking warriors.*

C *Another extract from the* Anglo-Saxon Chronicle.

921. King Edward went with a West Saxon army to Colchester, and repaired and rebuilt the fortress where it had been destroyed. Many people, both from East Anglia and from Essex, who had previously been under Danish rule, submitted to him: and the entire Danish host in East Anglia swore union with him.

D *This poem, in the* Anglo-Saxon Chronicle, *describes the battle of Brunanburh. (The Olaf mentioned in the poem was the Viking leader.)*

All through the day West Saxon horsemen
Pressed on in pursuit of the hostile peoples,
Fiercely, with swords sharpened on grindstones,
They cut down the Vikings as they fled.
Nor did the Mercians refuse hard fighting
To any of Olaf's warriors, who invaded
Our land . . .
Five young kings, slain by the sword,
Lay on the field, also seven
Of Olaf's earls, and a countless host
Of seamen and Scots. There the prince
Of the Norsemen, compelled by necessity,
Was forced to flee to the prow of his ship
With a handful of men. In haste the ship
Was launched, and the king fled hence
Over the waters grey, to save his life . . .
Never before in this island, as the books
Of ancient historians tell us, was an army
Put to greater slaughter by the sword . . .

Activities

1 Match the pairs in lists A and B.

List A	List B
Ruled Wessex 871–899 AD	Athelstan
Son of Alfred the Great	Aethelflaed
Daughter of Alfred the Great	Edward
He won at Brunanburh	Edgar
Ruled England 959–975 AD	Alfred

2 Read source A. In no more than four sentences write down how the Viking King Guthrum might have described the events of 878 AD.

3 a) Read source C. Why do you think King Edward rebuilt the fortress at Colchester?
b) Explain why the people from Essex and East Anglia might have been pleased to accept Edward as king.
c) Why do you think the Danes agreed to join with Edward?

4 Look at sources B and D. You are a Viking who has survived the battle of Brunanburh. Write down what you might have told a friend about the battle.

5 Work in groups. Try to list five reasons why the kings of Wessex conquered Danelaw in the 10th century rather than the Danish kings conquering Wessex. Choose someone to give your reasons to the rest of the class.

10 Viking Expansion

The Vikings invaded France, Ireland, Wales and Scotland as well as England. What effect did they have on these areas?

France was raided by Vikings for much of the 9th century. But by the 10th century, the French had built **fortified** bridges across major rivers. These held up Viking ships and gave the French time to raise armies. Many French soldiers were now trained to fight on horseback. This gave them an advantage in battle. Soon there were fewer Viking attacks on France.

In 911 AD a Viking army led by Rolf, or Rollo, invaded Normandy. Rolf was not very successful, but Charles the Simple, the French king, thought that he could make use of the Vikings. He made Rolf Duke of Normandy. In return, Rolf agreed to fight for Charles and defend Normandy from further Viking attack.

Rolf and his men quickly settled down in Normandy. They became Christian and were soon more French than Viking. Rolf's successors were to make the Normans a force to be reckoned with in 11th-century Europe.

In the 8th and 9th centuries Norwegian Vikings took over the Shetland, Faroe and Orkney islands, the Hebrides and the Isle of Man. These were good, easy-to-defend bases and most of the islands were ruled by the Vikings until well into the Middle Ages.

Ireland was a good target for the Vikings. It was weak and divided and had many rich churches. By 950 AD the Vikings had set up several bases, including Dublin and Cork. These soon became important trading towns – to the benefit of the whole of Ireland.

But from the start, many Irish did not like the new settlers and slowly but surely Irish kings won back control over the Viking areas. In 980 AD the Irish killed a large number of Vikings in Dublin. In 1014 the Irish High King, Brian Boru,

Viking settlements.

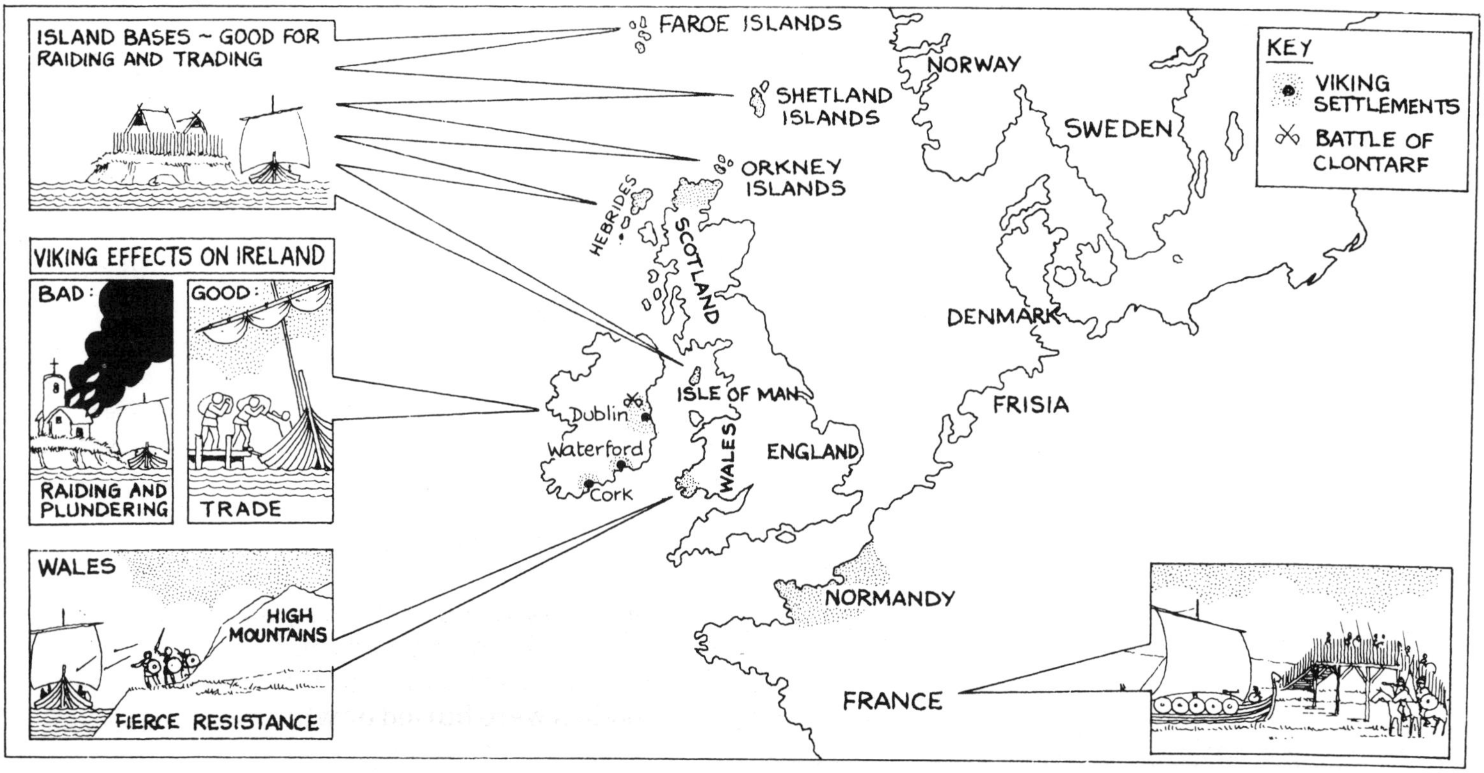

defeated a host of Vikings and Irish rebels at Clontarf. Brian was killed in the battle but the Vikings were never again a real force in Ireland.

In the 9th and 10th centuries, Irish Vikings often attacked Wales. But the Welsh fiercely resisted Viking settlement and Wales was never seriously invaded. A few Vikings did settle in south-west Wales.

A *An aerial photograph of Birsay in the Orkneys. In the Viking Age this island was the main base of the Earls of Orkney who fought in many of the larger Viking battles in Britain from the 9th to the 11th century.*

B *The skeletons of a man and a woman were found by archaeologists excavating a Viking house in Dublin. The two bodies had been buried in a shallow grave in the floor of the house. Buried near the skeletons were two gold armlets and a Viking coin, minted in 941 AD. A pile of human skulls was also found. One of the skulls had a sword wound in it.*

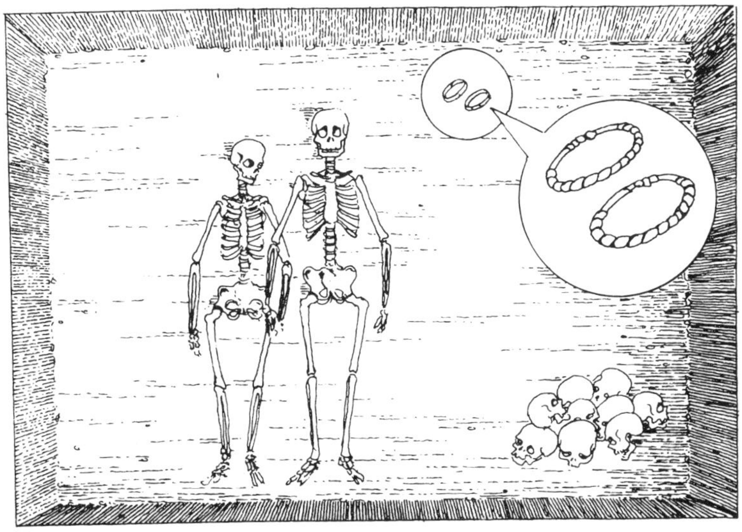

C *An extract from the* Annals of Ulster, *an Irish chronicle.*

The sea vomited a flood of foreigners over Ireland, so that no harbour, no beach, no town, fort, or castle could be found that survived the waves of Vikings and pirates . . . and they ravaged her kingdoms and her churches.

D *An account by William of Jumièges describes what happened when King Charles the Simple of France granted territory in Normandy to the Viking leader Rollo. This story was written over 150 years after the event.*

When the time came for Rollo to be created Duke . . . the bishops said to him, 'When you receive the honour, you must kneel and kiss the King's foot.' Rollo replied, 'I have never bowed before any man, let alone kiss his foot.' Finally he gave way to the pleadings of the Franks [French] and commanded one of his men to kiss the King's foot. The Northman bent down and, seizing the royal foot, stood up to kiss it, throwing the King on his back amid roars of laughter.

Activities

1 Look at the map. Why do you think the Faroes, Orkneys and Shetland islands were under Viking control for a long time?

2 a) Look at source A. Why might the Vikings have thought this a good place to set up a strong base?
b) What difficulties might they have had in setting up a base here?

3 Read source C. Does the chronicler like or dislike the Vikings? How do you know?

4 a) Read source D. Do you think this is reliable evidence? Explain your answer.
b) If the account is true, what do you think it shows about the Vikings?
c) What do you think the French King's feelings were about what happened?

5 a) Look at source B. Why do you think the two gold armlets were buried?
b) Can you think of any reasons why the two bodies were buried or why there might be a pile of skulls in the house?

11 The Settlement of Iceland and Greenland

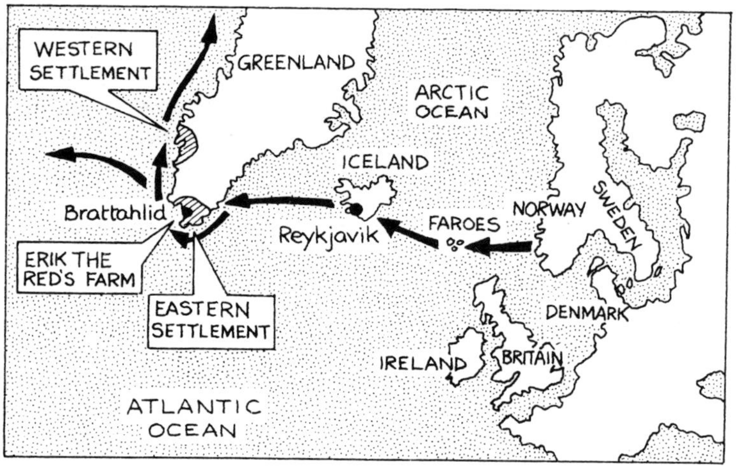

Iceland and Greenland.

In 860 AD no less than three Viking voyages of exploration found an island far to the north of Scotland. One explorer, Flokki Vigerdason, didn't like the look of the island and called it Iceland. But others said that there was plenty of land waiting for those brave enough to sail there.

In 874 AD, a group of Vikings led by Ingolf Arnarson left Norway for Iceland. Ingolf finally settled at Reykjavik (today the capital of Iceland). More and more Vikings followed Ingolf. By 950 AD there were probably 50,000 Viking settlers on Iceland and all the best land had been taken.

Soon after 900 AD a Viking called Gunbjorn sighted a new land far to the west of Iceland. At the end of the 10th century another Viking, Erik the Red, finally made use of Gunbjorn's find.

Erik was a trouble-maker. He was outlawed from Norway for killing some men. He fled to Iceland, killed more men and was outlawed again. He now sailed west and found the land that Gunbjorn had seen. Erik called it Greenland. He hoped that this name might persuade settlers to come to the new land.

He was successful. In 985 AD, 25 ships sailed from Iceland to Greenland carrying new settlers. Although only 14 of the ships completed the journey, there were soon enough Vikings to set up two main settlements.

Greenland was not very pleasant. It was cold for much of the year and farming was difficult. There was no wood or iron and Greenland was also cut off from Europe. Even Iceland was four days' sailing away in good weather.

But for most of the 11th and 12th centuries the Greenlanders survived and even prospered. The weather was a bit warmer then than now so they were able to grow crops and feed their animals. They got plenty of fish and whale and seal meat from the sea and sold furs and ivory to Europe.

Viking ships carrying settlers to Iceland and Greenland.

A *An extract from* The King's Mirror, *written in Iceland in the 13th century.*

It is reported that the land is good, and that there are large and fine farms in Greenland. The earth yields good and sweet-smelling grass. The farmers raise cattle and sheep in large numbers, and make butter and cheese in great quantities. The people exist chiefly on these foods, but they also eat the flesh of various kinds of game such as **caribou**, reindeer, whales, seals, and bears.

B *The farmhouse at Stong in Iceland. This was probably typical of Viking Age farms in Iceland.*

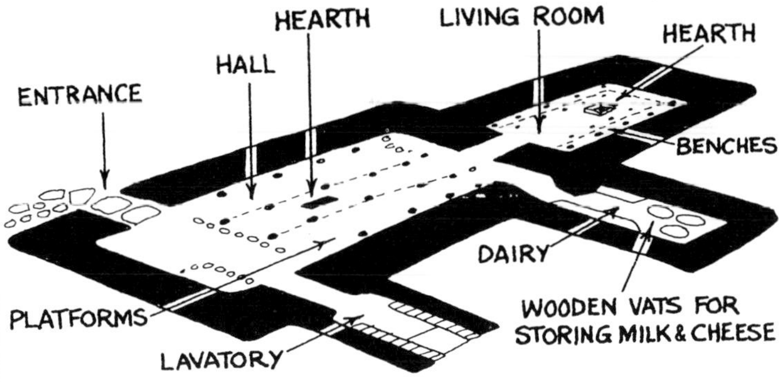

a) A ground plan.

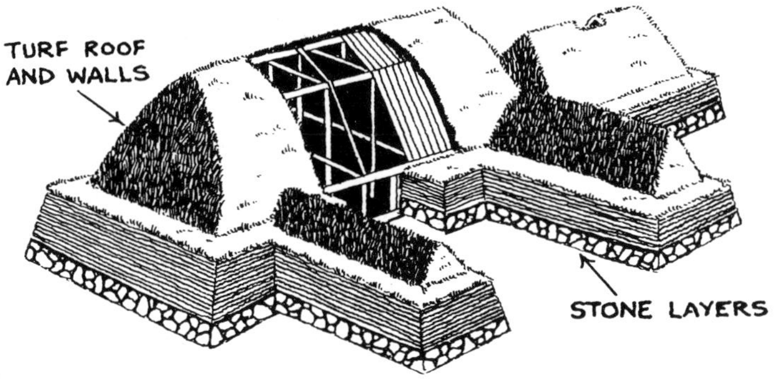

b) An architect's reconstruction of the outside of the farm.

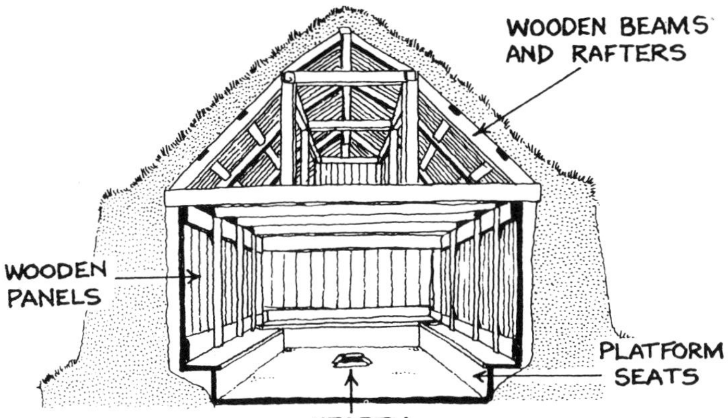

c) An architect's reconstruction of the inside of the small living-room at Stong.

C *This is from* Egil's Saga, *written in Iceland in the 13th century.*

King Harald Finehair took over all the land, all the seas and the rivers. Everyone now had to accept him as their lord, even those who lived in the forests or travelled about. Many people left Norway to get away from this, and so many new lands were settled. People went to the Hebrides, Ireland, Dublin, Normandy in France, Caithness in Scotland, the Orkneys, Shetland and the Faroes. And it was now that Iceland was discovered.

D *Ari the Wise wrote this in a history of Iceland in the early 12th century.*

Iceland was first settled from Norway in the days of Harald Fairhair, son of Halfdan the Black according to Teit my foster-father . . . and my uncle Thorkel Gellisson who remembered far back, and of Thurid daughter of Snorri who was both learned in many things and trustworthy . . . 870 years after the birth of Christ. A Norwegian called Ingolf, it is reliably reported, first went to Iceland when Harald Fairhair was 16 winters old, and for the second time a few winters later.

Activities

1 Why was each of the following men important in the history of Iceland and Greenland? Flokki Vigerdason; Ingolf Arnarson; Gunbjorn; Erik the Red.

2 a) Read sources C and D. According to source C why did some Vikings leave Norway to settle in Iceland?
b) In what way do sources C and D agree and disagree?
c) Which source do you think is the most reliable and why?

3 Look at source B. The farmhouse at Stong is up for sale. How might Viking estate agents have described the property? You should mention the material from which the house is made, how many rooms it has and why it is attractive and worth buying.

4 Read source A. Draw a travel poster trying to persuade Vikings from Iceland and Norway to settle in Greenland.

5 Work in groups. You are an Icelandic family about to sail to Greenland. You have two ships, similar to the ones shown on page 24. Decide how many people you think can go with you, including slaves. What else will you need to take with you? Explain your decisions to the other groups.

12 The Vikings Reach America

Viking discoveries did not end with Greenland. Most historians think that the Vikings were the first Europeans to reach America – 500 years before Columbus!

The first Viking to sight America was Bjarni Herjolfsson in 985 AD. Bjarni had been trying to sail from Iceland to Greenland but had been blown off course. He did not try to land but when he finally reached Greenland he told the settlers there of what he had seen.

In 1000 AD, Leif the Lucky, son of Erik the Red, sailed west from Greenland, hoping to find the new land. He finally came to a place that he called 'Vinland' or Wineland. It was a pleasant spot with good grass and wild fruits. Leif and his men made camp and stayed over the winter. Next spring they returned to Greenland with news of their discovery.

A few years later, Thorfinn Karlsefni took 160 men, women and children, hoping to settle in the new land. He found Leif's camp and spent two winters there. But Thorfinn then began to have trouble with Indians, or Skraelings as they were called. After several Indian attacks, the Vikings decided to return to Greenland.

Thorfinn Karlsefni.

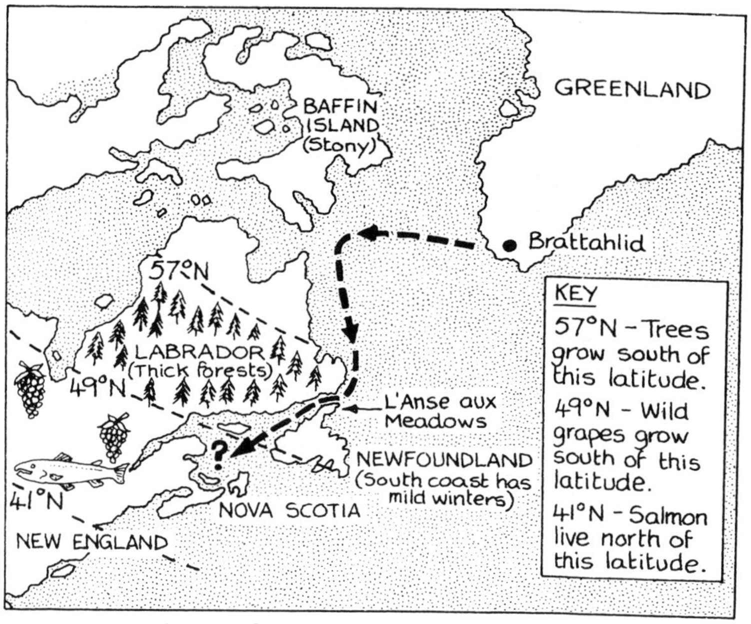

Leif Erikson's route?

Just where Leif and Thorfinn landed remains a mystery. Various places in America have claimed to be Vinland and people have claimed to have found Viking objects in many parts of North America. Almost all these objects have turned out to be forgeries.

Quite recently Norwegian archaeologists discovered what seems very likely to have been a Viking settlement at L'Anse aux Meadows in Northern Newfoundland.

But it is unlikely that this is the Vinland site of Leif. It is not even certain that the settlement is Viking! It is still possible that the stories of Leif and Thorfinn are just fiction, made up by a Viking storyteller many hundreds of years ago.

In some ways it is surprising that the Vikings did not make more effort to settle in America, which was much more pleasant and fertile than Greenland. Distance, lack of numbers and the Indian threat seem to have beaten them. By the 15th century, few if any Europeans had any idea that the Vikings had reached America.

A The Greenlanders Saga *(written in about 1300).*

There was now great talk [in Greenland] of discovering new countries. Leif, the son of Erik the Red of Brattahlid, went to see Bjarni Herjolfsson and bought his ship off him and engaged a crew of 35.

B The Greenlanders Saga.

The first land that they found was like one great slab of rock. The country seemed worthless. Leif said . . . 'Now I will give this country a name, and call it Helluland' (the land of flat stone).

They put to sea again and sighted a second shore. They sailed close in to it, dropped anchor, lowered a boat and went ashore. This land was flat and wooded, with white sandy beaches. Then Leif said, 'This land will be named after what grows here. It shall be called Markland' (Forest Land).

They sailed south-west for two days before they sighted land again. They beached their ship at a place where a river ran out of a lake. There were plenty of salmon in the river and the lake, bigger salmon than they had ever seen before. They decided to spend the winter there and built large houses. There was no frost all winter.

In the spring they got ready to leave. The ship's boat was filled with grapes. They also had a full cargo of timber. Leif named the country after the things that grew there and called it 'Vinland'.

C The Saga of Erik the Red.

That spring, Karlsefni and his men sailed a long way down the coast until they came to a river . . . Here they found wild wheat growing on the low ground and grape vines on the high ground. Every stream was full of fish . . . They built their homes above the lake: some of their houses were near the waterside, and others further away. They spent the winter there. No snow fell and all their livestock were able to graze . . .

Then early one morning, they saw nine skin-canoes approaching. The men in them were waving sticks . . . The new arrivals rowed ashore . . . They were dark-skinned, ugly men who wore their hair in a strange fashion. They had large eyes and broad cheekbones. They began to trade. What the natives liked most of all was red cloth. They also wanted to buy swords and spears but Thorfinn would not sell.

After that there was no sign of the savages for three weeks. But then Thorfinn's men saw a great many boats coming from the south. This time all the savages were howling. There was a fierce battle. Two of the Northmen were killed and four of the savages.

D *Plan of the site at L'Anse aux Meadows.*

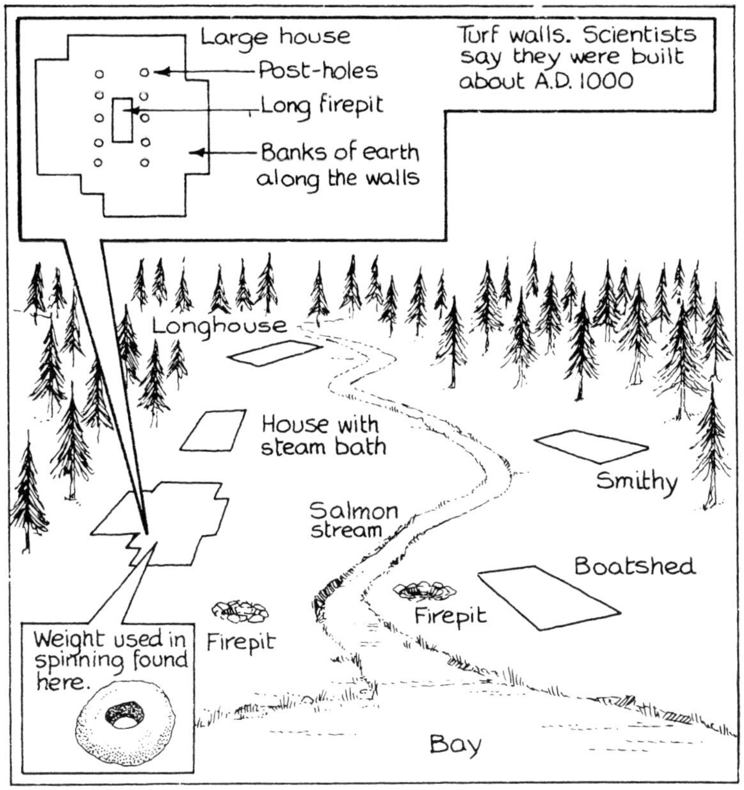

Activities

1 a) Read source A. Who was Bjarni Herjolfsson?
b) Some historians think that Leif sailed to America by accident. Does this source support that view or not? Give reasons.

2 Read source B. Why do you think it is difficult to find Vinland today from this description?

3 Look at source D. List all the things found at L'Anse aux Meadows which suggest that it was a Viking settlement.

4 Read sources B and C. Divide the class into four groups. Thorfinn has called a meeting to decide whether to stay in Vinland or return home. Two groups should make out a case for staying in Vinland. The other two groups should make out a case for leaving Vinland and returning to Greenland.

13 Viking Traders

Vikings are better known for raiding rather than trading. Yet many Vikings preferred trading to raiding. It was less risky and just as profitable.

Scandinavia was rich in furs, timber and fish but it did not produce fine cloth, good wine and other luxury goods. Viking traders swapped goods with merchants all over Europe, hoping to make a profit as they did so.

There was no proper money in Scandinavia until the 11th century. Gold and silver, however, were valued. Viking traders often carried a set of scales so that they could weigh the gold and silver that they were exchanging. But often Vikings would simply barter, trading one thing for something else.

There were several important trading towns in Scandinavia in the Viking Age, including Hedeby and Birka. Goods from all over the world have been found in both these towns.

Some Viking merchants went west, bringing prosperity to towns like York and Dublin. In Viking times both towns contained many wooden houses, warehouses and workshops and had many different types of craftsmen, including woodworkers, jewellers and potters.

Other Viking traders sailed eastwards across the Baltic Sea, visiting lands that are now part of Russia. They went to great lengths to trade, often pulling their ships for many miles overland so that they could sail down great rivers like the Dneiper and the Volga, into the heart of Russia.

Some Vikings settled in towns like Novgorod and Kiev. They were known as the Rus and some set themselves up as rulers over the Slav people who had lived in the area long before the Vikings arrived.

Some Viking traders went even further than Russia, travelling south to the great city of Constantinople and east to the Caspian Sea. They knew that many goods like silks and spices could only be found in these areas.

Viking trade routes

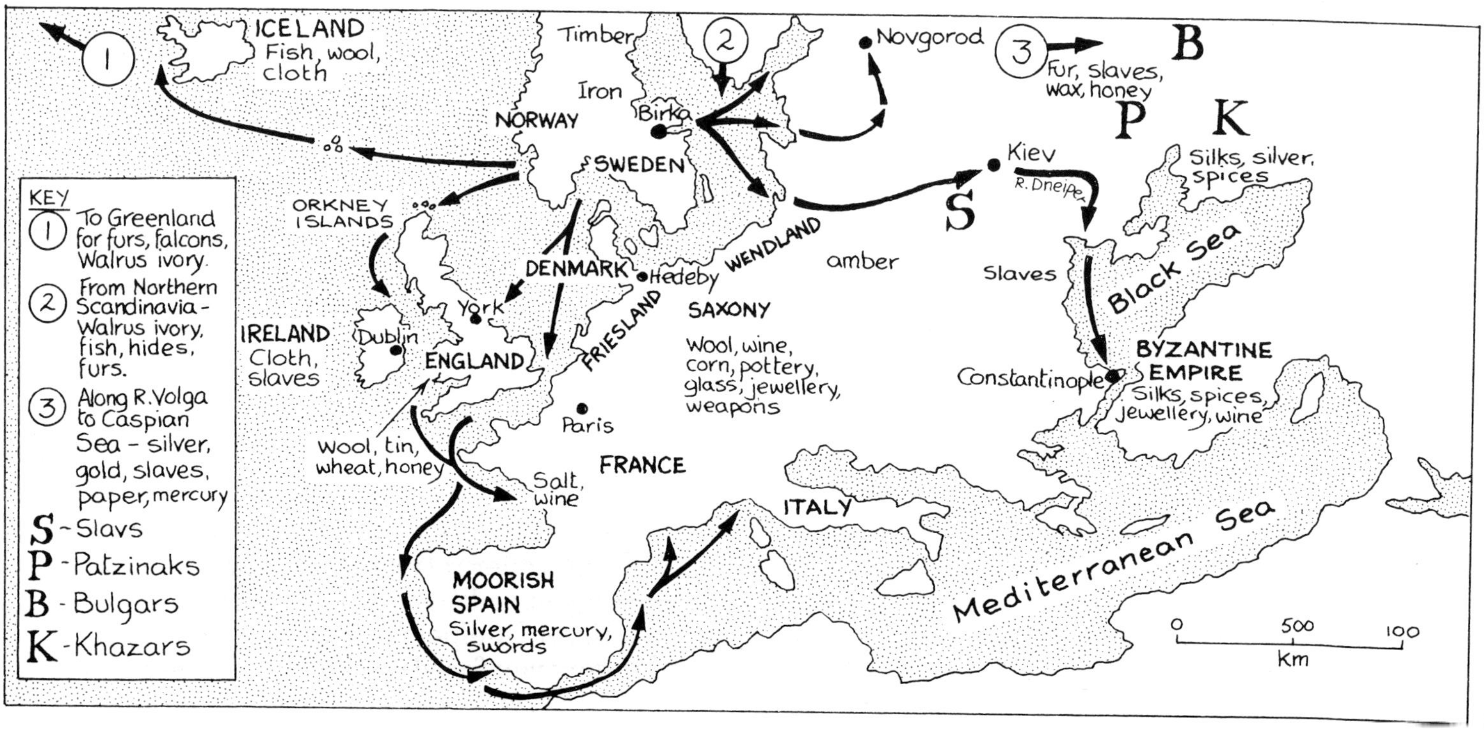

Trading was not always easy or peaceful. Viking merchants risked the loss of their goods through shipwreck or robbery and had to be ready to fight to defend their property.

A *An extract from* Egil's Saga, *written in Iceland in the 13th century. (Thorolf was a Norwegian Viking).*

Thorolf got his ship ready and loaded it with dried fish, skins, coarse cloth and furs. It was a rich cargo. He went south along the coast, turned towards the open sea, and reached England. He traded well, loaded the ship with wheat, honey, wine and good cloth, and came back in the autumn.

B *An artist's impression of what Hedeby may have been like in the Viking Age.*

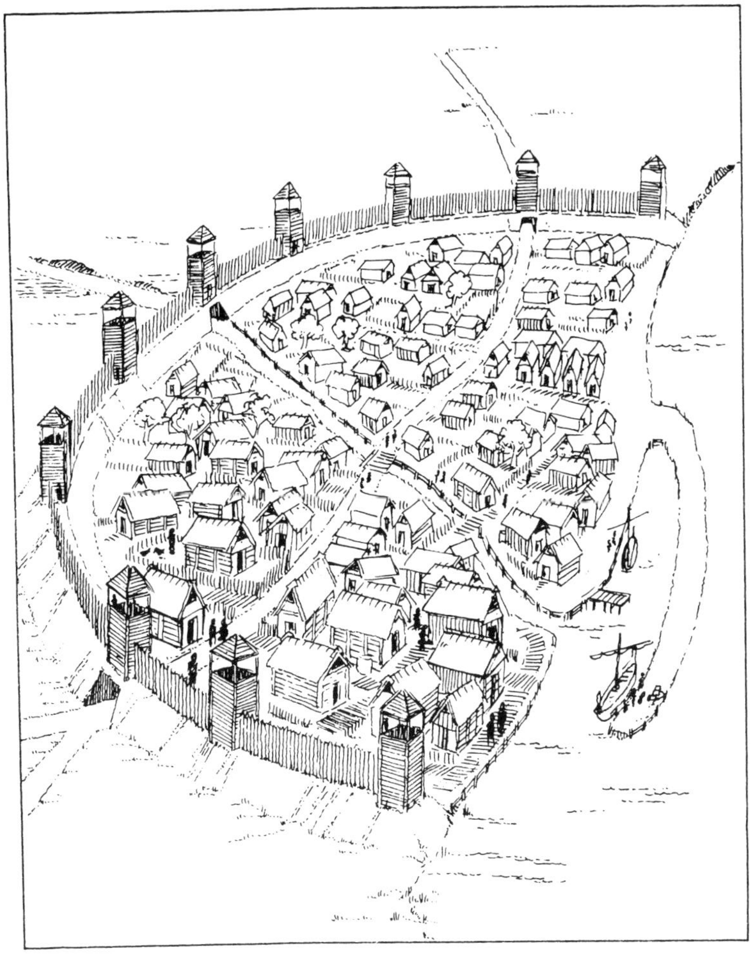

C *Ibn Fadlan, an Arab, describes his meeting with some Vikings on the river Volga in 922 AD.*

Each man has a couch on which he sits. With him are pretty slave girls intended for sale to merchants ... The Viking says ... 'I have such and such a number of girls and such a number of furs' and he lists the rest of his goods.

D *Ibn Rustah, writing in 920 AD, describes how the Rus of Kiev lived at that time.*

They fight with the Slavs and use ships to attack them; they take them captive and carry them to the Khazars and there they sell them as slaves ... They have no villages, states or fields. Their only occupation is trading in squirrel and other kinds of skins, which they sell to those who will buy from them.

E *This is from a book written in 950 AD by the Byzantine Emperor of Constantinople for his son.*

At the fourth great set of rapids [on the river Dneiper] ... the Vikings bring their ships to land. They then send men into the surrounding countryside to look out for the Patzinaks, their enemies, who are always waiting to ambush them. They unload the ships and march their slaves in chains across land for six miles. The boats are then lifted out of the water and half carried, half dragged overland. Once past the rapids, they lower them once more into the water, load them with their goods and sail off again.

Activities

1 Look at the map on page 28. If you were a Viking merchant from Hedeby, to which parts of Europe might you have to go to get the following goods: amber; walrus ivory; silks; weapons; glass; slaves?

2 Read source A. Make lists of the things which Thorolf sold in England and the things that he bought there.

3 Look at source B. Describe the main features of the town.

4 a) Read sources C and D. In what ways do they agree?
b) Nowadays slavery seems a bad thing. Does this mean that the Vikings who sold slaves were all bad men? Explain your answer.

5 Read source E and look at the map. You are a Viking trader returning to Hedeby after a trading expedition to Constantinople down the River Dneiper. Write a report on the dangers you faced on the journey. Mention also what you bought, sold and exchanged.

14 Viking Society

Although some Scandinavians went on Viking voyages, most stayed at home. Their lives depended on how rich they were and whether they were male or female.

The most important people in the Viking world were kings and their families. In the 9th century there were many kings ruling small areas of land. They owned large halls and many slaves and had rich possessions. But they had to be careful. They might lose their land to stronger enemies. They might also be murdered by members of their own family!

Next in importance were the jarls or earls. Some owned great amounts of land and were as rich and powerful as kings. But many were far less wealthy, owning just one hall and a few slaves.

Most Scandinavians were farmers earning a living from small plots of land. They grew crops like oats, barley and wheat, and kept some animals – sheep, cattle, goats and horses. Some were skilled craftsmen such as blacksmiths and woodcarvers.

At the bottom of society were the slaves. Some were slaves because their parents had been slaves. Others had been prisoners or criminals. Some had sold themselves as slaves in order to pay off a debt.

Slaves had few rights and were usually given the nastiest jobs. Some were badly treated. Others were treated well and sometimes looked on almost as members of their owner's family.

Women played a vital role in Scandinavian life. Wives of nobles protected their lands and controlled the slaves when their husbands were away. Wives of farmers spent much of their time helping on the farm, preparing food, and spinning and weaving.

Scandinavian women enjoyed more freedom than most women in Europe in the Viking Age. They could own land and divorce their husbands if they wished. Even so, for most women in Viking times, life was a constant round of household chores and child-rearing.

A *An artist's impression of what a Scandinavian kitchen may have looked like.*

B *In a poem, the* Rigsthula, *a 12th-century Swedish poet described the different kinds of people in Scandinavia in the Viking Age.*

Karl was red-haired, red-faced and bright-eyed. Eagerly he set to work, taming oxen, making ploughs and carts, building timber houses and barns, and ploughing . . .

Thrall was black and ugly with rough hands . . . His back was hunched and his feet flat. Thrall was set to work building fences, manuring fields, tending pigs, guarding goats and digging **peat**. The whole day long he carried great loads of firewood . . .

Earl's hair was blond, his cheeks bright and his eyes as fierce as a young serpent's . . . As he grew up Earl learned how to throw spears, string a bow, ride on horseback, hunt with hounds, brandish swords and do feats of swimming.

C *The following account describes a wealthy 11th-century Norwegian chieftain.*

Erling always had 30 slaves at home on his farm, besides other servants. He would allot the day's work to his slaves, but after this would give them their time free, with permission to every man who so wished to work for himself in the evening. He gave them lands to sow corn for themselves, and let them use the crop for their own profit.

He would set a certain amount of work to each, to win himself freedom by doing it; and there were many who earned their freedom in this way in one year, or in the second year, and all who had any capacity for work could make themselves free within three years. With this money Erling bought other slaves.

D *An extract from* Erik's Saga.

Sybil wore a blue dress fastened with straps and covered with jewels all the way down to the hem. She had a necklace of glass beads. On her head she wore a black lambskin hood lined with white cat's fur. On her feet she wore hairy calfskin shoes with long thick laces which had large tin buttons on the end. She wore catskin gloves with white fur inside.

Activities

1 a) Read source B. List the ways in which the different groups spent their days.
b) To which of the groups – noble, free farmer, or slave – did Karl, Thrall and Earl belong?

2 Read source C. Do you think Erling was wise or foolish to treat his slaves in this way? Explain your answer.

3 a) Look at source A. How is the room lit?
b) What cooking items are the women using?
c) Why was preparing food more a chore in Viking times than today?

4 a) Read source D. To which group in Viking society do you think Sybil belonged and why?
b) Using the information in the source, draw and label a picture of Sybil.

15 Life in Scandinavia in Viking Times

By today's standards, life in Scandinavia in Viking times was not very pleasant. Most people lived on small farms and had to make most of what they needed for themselves. Many lived in one-roomed, wooden houses that they shared with farm animals. The houses had no drains, no running water, no windows and no chimneys.

Viking Scandinavia was also a dangerous place. There were many thieves and outlaws and no police. Families often took their own revenge on someone whom they thought had committed a crime. This led to bitter family feuds which could go on for many years.

Some European countries were probably richer and more civilised than Scandinavia. But in many ways, life in Scandinavia in the Viking Age was not very different to life elsewhere in Europe. And in some ways the Vikings were more advanced than other Europeans. Many Vikings, for example, were excellent craftsmen and artists. They were certainly the best shipbuilders in Europe.

Viking houses were not all one-roomed barns. They came in all shapes and sizes and were often skilfully built. Rich Vikings often lived in large, finely decorated halls. These halls were often used for great feasts.

The Vikings cared a great deal about their personal appearance. They washed regularly, wore brightly-coloured clothes and as much jewellery as they could afford. They enjoyed their leisure time, playing games like chess and taking part in sports like wrestling and archery.

The Vikings were not completely lawless. A meeting of all the people in an area – the Thing – made laws and passed sentences. Those found guilty of a crime usually had to pay compensation to the family who had suffered from the crime. Criminals were sometimes enslaved, **banished** from an area or outlawed. Anyone was allowed to kill an outlaw.

A man accused of a crime could clear himself if enough of his friends swore he was innocent. The Vikings also used trial by ordeal. An accused person might have to pick up stones from boiling water. If badly scalded, he or she was found guilty.

Although the Vikings had few great scholars, they did have some great poets who recited poems and songs from memory. Many Vikings were also able to read and write. They used the Runic rather than the Roman alphabet.

A feast in a Viking hall.

A *An artist's impression of a typical Scandinavian farm.*

B *Ibrahim ibn Ahmed at-Tartushi, an Arab trader from Spain, described a visit to Hedeby in the 950s AD.*

There's not much in the way of goods or wealth there. People mainly eat fish, because there's so much of it. When a child is born, it is often thrown into the sea to save the trouble of bringing it up. Women can just say whenever they want to divorce their husbands and then they leave. Both men and women use make-up for their eyes – and as long as they go on using it they look handsome. Their singing sounds horrible, the worst in the world. It's like a growl coming out of their throats, or like dogs barking – but much more beastly.

C *The Runic alphabet.*

D *This saga story describes how Frith, a king's daughter, welcomed Bui, a freeman from Iceland.*

She drew up a fair table, and laid it. Then she carried to him a silver basin and costly towel, and afterwards asked him to eat and drink. She fetched in delicious food and splendid drink. All of the table things, dishes, goblets and spoons, were of silver decorated with gold.

Activities

1 a) Look at source A. Draw the Scandinavian farm and label the following buildings: hall, smithy, boathouse, toilet.
b) What do you think the other buildings may have been used for?

2 a) Read source B. In what way does this source suggest that the Vikings were not very civilised?
b) Does this source prove that the Vikings were not very civilised? Explain your answer.

3 a) Look at source C. Why do you think the Runic letters were all made from straight lines?
b) Write your name using the Runic alphabet.

4 Look at source D and the picture on the opposite page. You have been invited to a feast in the hall of a Viking chieftain. Describe what it is like.

5 In groups, try to decide what were the good and bad things about life in Scandinavia in Viking times. Explain the reasoning behind your decisions to the other groups.

16 Jorvik

A thousand years ago York was the capital of the North of England. It was also one of the greatest trading ports in Europe. A monk at that time said it was packed with people, rich goods, and traders 'from all parts, especially Danes'. York owed its **prosperity** to the hard work and trading skill of the Vikings. These new settlers called the town Jorvik.

The Vikings captured York in 866 AD. They controlled the city until the mid-10th century. The last Viking ruler of York was called Eric Blood-Axe.

The Vikings changed the way of life in York. They introduced many of their own customs – language, dress, art, crafts and industries. They repaired and extended Jorvik's walls and set out new streets. Many streets in York still end in 'gate' – an old Norse word meaning street.

Viking York has now disappeared. Most of Jorvik's buildings were made of wood. They have either been demolished, burnt down, or rotted away. But in some parts of York, archaeologists have found that remains of Jorvik still survive. They are buried deep below the streets of the modern city.

From 1976 until 1981 a large team of archaeologists dug up the site of one old Viking street, Coppergate. Some 15,000 small objects were found. Damp soils even preserved the remains of many timber buildings.

As a result of these discoveries the Viking street of Coppergate has been reconstructed at the Jorvik Viking Centre. There are models of Viking townspeople buying and selling, working and playing. Trolley cars carry visitors back in time into a world of Viking sights, sounds and smells.

A *A picture of a recreated Viking street in the Jorvik Viking Centre.*

B *Some of the Viking objects found in York.*

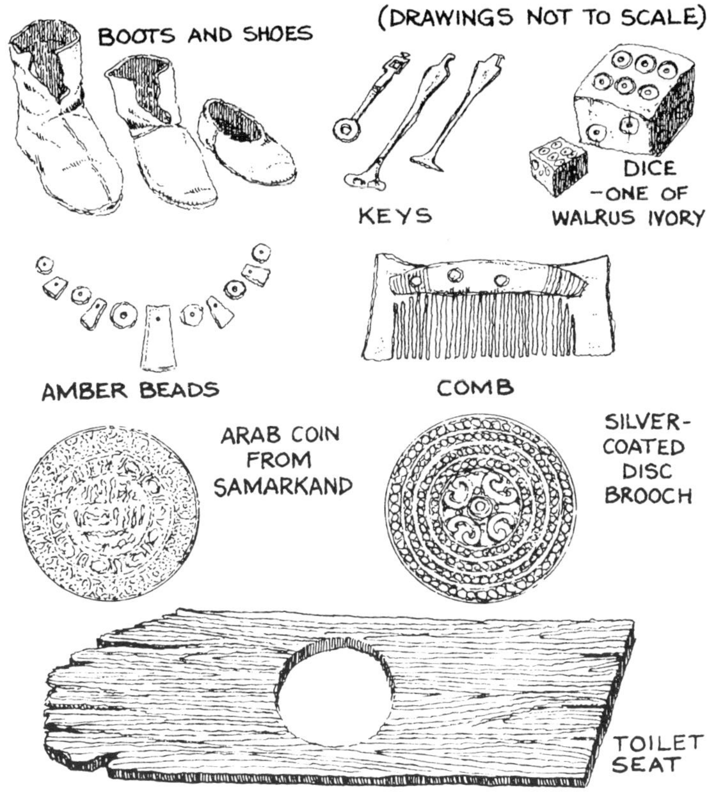

C *A photograph showing archaeologists at work in Coppergate, York.*

D *Pictures of some of the Viking people at work in Jorvik.*

A jeweller.

An antler worker and a woodturner's apprentice.

Activities

1 Look at source A. In four sentences describe how the Viking street is different from a city street today.

2 Look at source B. Which of these objects do you think is the most surprising thing to have been found? Explain the reasons for your choice.

3 Look at source C. Why do you think it took five years to excavate the Coppergate site?

4 Look at source D. Choose two of the characters. Write down an interview that you might have had with them. Ask them questions about their clothes, their jobs and the type of houses that they lived in.

17 Viking Religion

At the start of the Viking Age the Scandinavians were pagans, not Christians. They worshipped several gods. These gods were very similar to the old Anglo-Saxon gods. The two main gods were Odin (or Woden), god of War, Wisdom and Poetry, and Thor, god of the Sky. Other gods included Frey, Tyr, Balder and Loki. Freja was the goddess of Love.

According to Norse legends, the Vikings believed that their gods lived at a place called Asgard. Here they prepared for a last great battle against dragons, giants, wolves and evil men. In the middle of this battle the whole world, including the gods and monsters, would be destroyed. A new world would then arise and everyone would live happily ever afterwards!

Odin.

The Vikings certainly believed in life after death. Women were often buried in their best clothes and jewellery. Men were sometimes buried with their favourite weapon. Food and drink, which might be needed on the journey to the next life, were often buried with the dead. When rich Vikings died, slaves were sometimes killed and buried with them.

The Vikings believed that warriors who died bravely in battle went to Odin's hall at Valhalla. They were taken there by the Valkyries or battle maidens. At Valhalla, the warriors spent their time feasting and fighting in readiness for the last battle against the forces of evil. Those who did not go to Valhalla went to a dismal underworld called Hel.

The Vikings were keen to please their gods and offered sacrifices to them. Animals (especially horses) and people were killed.

Most of what we know about the old Viking religion comes from books that were written by Christians. Christian writers were often hostile to the old religion so just who and how the Vikings worshipped is still a bit of a mystery.

A *The* Saga of the Men of Keelness, *written in the 13th century.*

Thorgrimm was very keen on sacrifices. He had a great temple built in his home meadow . . . It was 30 metres long and 20 broad . . . Thor was the chief god there . . .

The temple was decorated with **tapestries** and had windows. Thor stood in the middle, with the other gods on each side. In front was an iron altar, made with great skill. There was a fire, which was never to go out, called a sacred fire. On the altar there was a large silver ring, for the temple priest to have on his hand at every meeting. There also was a great copper bowl into which ran the blood of the men and beasts sacrificed to Thor . . .

The men they sacrificed were thrown into the pool outside the door, which they called the well of sacrifice.

B *A 10th-century figure found in Iceland. Historians think it may represent the god Thor.*

C *Adam of Bremen, a German, wrote this around 1075.*

The Swedes have a very famous temple called Uppsala ... In this temple, completely covered with gold, are three idols which the Swedes worship: Thor, the mightiest god, has his throne in the middle of the hall, and Odin and Frey are on either side of him. Attached to the gods are priests who offer up sacrifices. If disease or famine threaten, they sacrifice to the idol Thor; if there is war, to Odin; and if a wedding is to be celebrated they sacrifice to Frey ...

The sacrifice is of this nature: nine male creatures of various species are offered ... The bodies are strung up in the wood that is closest to the temple ...

There dogs and cats hang beside human beings, and a Christian told me that he had seen 72 such bodies hanging all mixed up together. The songs that are sung during such a sacrifice are varied and shameful, therefore the less said about them the better.

D *Ibn Fadlan, an Arab diplomat, saw and described a Viking funeral in Russia in the 10th century.*

At last I was told of the death of one of their chief men ... The dead man's family asked his slave-girls, 'Who will die with him?' One answered, 'I will.' Then they gave two slave-girls the task of seeing to her and being with her wherever she went ...

When the day came for him and the girl to be burnt, I went to the river where his ship lay. It had been pulled up on to dry land and around it ... had been built a great stack of wood. Then an old woman arrived whom they call the Angel of Death ... She was a large old woman, stout and grim-looking ... They carried the dead man into a tent which stood on the ship ... Then they came with a dog, cut it into two halves and threw them into the ship ...

Now they took the slave-girl to the ship ... The old woman took her hand and made her enter the tent, and went in with her. Thereupon the men began to beat their shields with sticks so that her cries would not be heard and other girls would not be frightened and so refuse death with their masters ...

They laid her at her master's side. Two men held her feet and two her hand. The old woman ... looped a cord round her neck, and gave the crossed ends to two of the men to pull. Then she came forward with a broad-bladed dagger and plunged it over and over again between the girl's ribs, while the two men strangled her with the cord until she was dead.

Then the closest relative of the dead man came and took a piece of lighted wood ... and set fire to the pile of wood beneath the ship.

Activities

1 Match up the pairs in lists A and B.

List A	List B
Another name for Odin	Valkyrie
Home of the gods	Valhalla
God of the Sky	Asgard
A battle-maiden of Odin	Thor
Odin's hall	Woden

2 Read source A. From the description draw a plan of (a) the temple and (b) the altar.

3 Look at source B. Why do you think that archaeologists believe the figure is Thor?

4 a) Read source C. Do you think the writer was a Christian or a pagan? Give reasons for your answer.
b) Do you think that the writer had ever been to the temple at Uppsala? Give a reason for your answer.

5 a) Read source D. Why do you think the slave-girl was killed?
b) Why do you think she agreed to be sacrificed?
c) Draw strip pictures showing the main events in source D.

18 The Vikings Return to England

Tactics tried by Ethelred.

By the middle of the 10th century, the Viking threat to England seemed to be over. King Edgar (959-975 AD) had a peaceful reign. But his son Ethelred was not so lucky.

Ethelred is often thought to be one of the worst English rulers. He is usually nicknamed the 'Unready'. In the 11th century he was said to be 'unraed'. This meant not unready but 'badly advised' or 'unwise'. Perhaps he was unready, unwise and badly advised!

Ethelred became king in 978 AD after the murder of his brother Edward. He was only eleven years old. It was a bad time for anyone to become king. Viking raiders from Denmark began to attack England again – and again.

Ethelred and his advisers decided to pay the Vikings large sums of money to go away. This money, raised by taxes, was known as **Danegeld**. The tactic did not work. Instead more Vikings attacked England and Ethelred ended up paying more and more Danegeld.

Ethelred also raised large armies and fleets to defeat the Danes, but without much success. Local forces sometimes put up a brave fight but Ethelred was not much of a warrior and did not always select good men to fight for him.

In 1013, King Swein Fork-Beard of Denmark invaded England, planning to win the throne. He had many ships and men and many Englishmen accepted him. In 1014 Ethelred fled to Normandy. But five weeks later Swein died.

Ethelred returned to England and won back his throne. He died in 1016. By then Cnut, Swein's son, had invaded England hoping to become king.

Perhaps we should have some sympathy for Ethelred. He faced Viking attacks which were larger than those in Alfred the Great's time. Perhaps, in the end, he was more 'unlucky' than 'unready'. What do you think?

A *Extracts from the* Anglo-Saxon Chronicle.

991. It was decided for the first time to pay money to the Danes because of their **atrocities** along the coasts. The first payment was £10,000 . . .
994. The whole Viking force came to Southampton and there took up winter quarters. They were supplied by Ethelred and paid £16,000 . . .
1002. The King and his councillors decided to pay money to the Vikings on condition they stopped their evil deeds . . . They were paid £24,000.
1007. £36,000 was paid to the Vikings.

B *'Danegeld', a poem written by Rudyard Kipling, at the start of the 20th century.*

It is always a temptation to an armed and agile nation,
To call upon a neighbour and to say:
'We invaded you last night – we are quite prepared to fight,
Unless you pay us cash to go away.'

It is always a temptation to a rich and lazy nation,
To puff and look important and to say:
'Though we know we should defeat you, we have not the time to meet you.
We will therefore pay you cash to go away.'

And that is called paying the Dane-geld;
But we've proved it again and again,
That if once you have paid him the Dane-geld
You never get rid of the Dane . . .

So when you are requested to pay up or be molested [annoyed],
You will find it better policy to say:

'We never pay any one Dane-geld,
No matter how trifling the cost,
For the end of that game is oppression and shame,
And the nation that plays it is lost!'

C *A reconstruction of the fortress at Trelleborg in Denmark. This was one of four great fortresses all built around 980 AD to a very similar plan. The Trelleborg fortress could hold about 1,000 men. The largest fortress at Aggersborg could hold 3,000 men.*

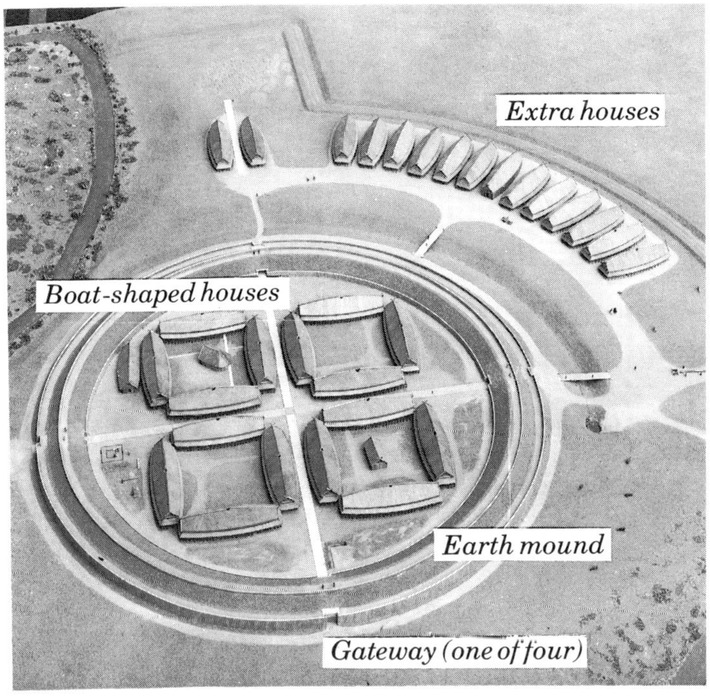

D *Further extracts from the* Anglo-Saxon Chronicle.

1010. And while the Danes were on their way back to their ships, the English army should have been out in case they tried to go inland; but our men were on their way home instead. And when the enemy was in the east, our men were in the west; and when the enemy was in the south, our soldiers were in the north . . . Whatever course of action was decided upon, it was not followed even for a single month . . .
1011. All the disasters were the result of bad policy, in that the enemy were never offered payment in time, nor fought against; but when they had done their worst, only then was peace made with them. Yet for all the payments and the peace treaties, they went about everywhere in bands, attacking, robbing and slaying our wretched people . . . Then they besieged Canterbury . . . And there they seized the Archbishop Aelfheah . . . and they kept the Archbishop as their prisoner . . .
1012 . . . The Vikings became very angry with Archbishop Aelfheah because he was not willing to offer them any money, and forbade any **ransom** to be given for him. Moreover they were very drunk . . . Then they took the Archbishop . . . and pelted him to death with the bones and skulls of dead cattle.

Activities

1 a) Read sources A and B. In what way does source A support the main idea of source B?
b) Do you agree with the point that source B is making? Explain your answer.

2 a) Look at source C. You are an English spy. Send a report to King Ethelred describing the Trelleborg fortress.
b) What does this source tell us about the strength of the Danish kings in the late 10th century?

3 a) Read source D. Why is the writer of the Chronicle critical of Ethelred?
b) Do you think Archbishop Aelfheah was brave or foolish? Explain your answer.

4 Work in groups. You are Ethelred's counsellors. What advice would you give him to try to defeat the Viking threat?

5 Which nickname do you think Ethelred deserves – unready, badly advised, unwise or unlucky? Give reasons for your answer.

19 King Cnut

In 1016 two men claimed the English throne. One was Edmund Ironside, son of Ethelred the Unready. The other was Cnut, son of Swein Fork-Beard. They fought a series of battles before agreeing to divide England between them. But within a month Edmund died. Cnut, now accepted as king by most English nobles, became the first Viking ruler of all England.

Cnut ruled England from 1016 to 1035. Few people today know much about him. Only one story about him is famous. He is supposed to have sat on his throne on a beach and ordered the incoming tide to go back – without success. His aim was to show that he was not all-powerful. But this story was not written down until many years after Cnut's death and is only a legend.

Cnut may not have ruled the waves but he certainly ruled a great Viking empire which included England, Norway and Denmark. What type of king was he? Was he a good and successful ruler? Or was he a Viking thug who ruled with the help of a gang of pirates?

Cnut could be brutal and totally ruthless. One of his first actions was to hunt down Eadwig, Edmund Ironside's brother and have him killed. Other Anglo-Saxon princes fled abroad, fearing what Cnut might do to them.

At first Cnut's main advisers were Danish, and many Danes were given huge grants of land in England. In 1018 he raised a massive tax of £82,500 to pay off the Viking army and fleet which had brought him to power.

But Cnut also did everything he could to please his English subjects. He tried to rule like previous English kings. After 1018 he raised no more heavy taxes. Most of his advisers were Englishmen. Soon Cnut regarded England as the centre of his empire. He spent more time in England than anywhere else.

Cnut was Christian and ruled England with the help of his abbots and bishops. He gave rich gifts to almost all the main churches. In 1027 he even went on a **pilgrimage** to Rome.

In 1017 he married Ethelred's widow, Emma of Normandy, despite the fact that he was already married to Aelgifu of Northampton. Surprisingly, the fact that he had two wives does not seem to have worried many clergymen!

Cnut seems to have been a strong and respected king. He gave England many years of peace. The country was no longer threatened by Vikings. Instead, Englishmen fought in Norway and Denmark against Cnut's enemies.

Cnut died in England in 1035 and was buried in Winchester like a normal Anglo-Saxon king. His sons Harold and Harthacnut ruled England until 1042. But then Edward the Confessor, son of Ethelred the Unready, became king. Viking rule in England was over.

King Cnut.

A *Extracts from the* Anglo-Saxon Chronicle.

1014. Cnut put to sea with his fleet . . . he sailed southward until he came to the port of Sandwich, and there put ashore the hostages which had been given to his father, and cut off their hands, ears and noses . . .

1016. In this year came Cnut with 160 ships and with him Earl Eadric, and they crossed the River Thames into Mercia . . . and then turned into Warwickshire and in that county during the Christmas season they burned and slew all that they found.

B *A family tree showing the Saxon and Danish kings in the 11th century.*

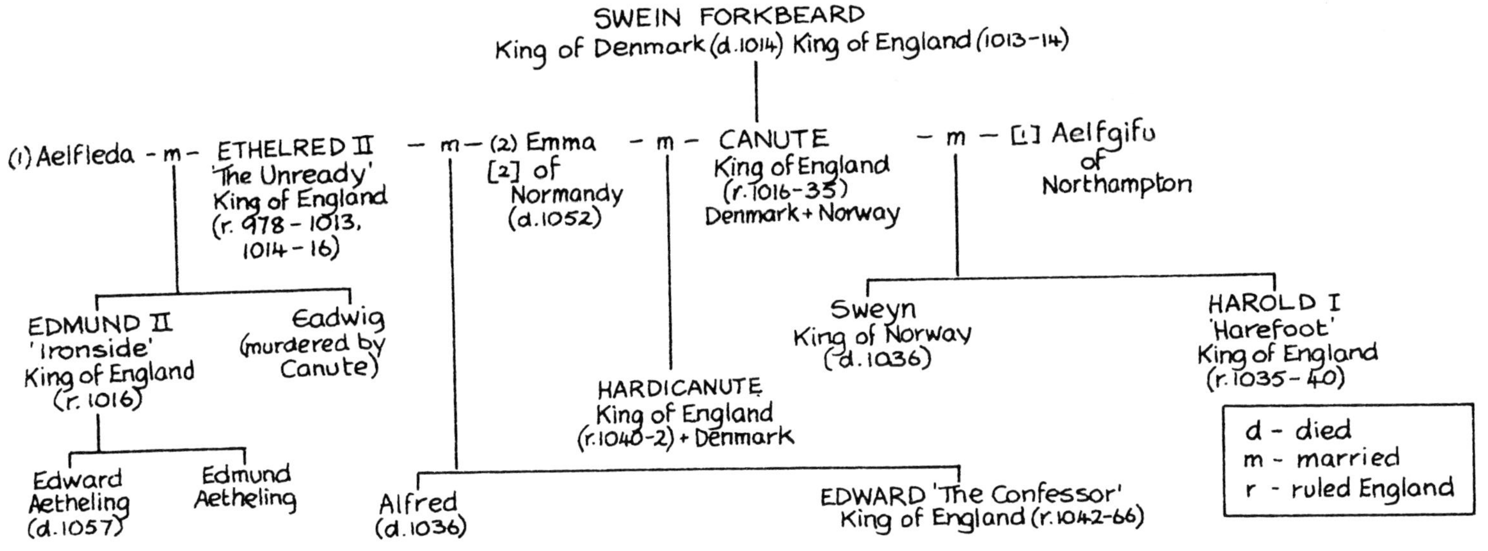

C *Another extract from the* Anglo-Saxon Chronicle.

1018. In this year the people of England had to pay a tax of £72,000; in addition the citizens of London had to pay £10,500. Many of Cnut's forces returned to Denmark, and 40 ships remained with King Cnut. And Danes and English came to an agreement at Oxford to observe the laws of King Edgar.

D *Cnut and Queen Emma, presenting an altar-cross to Winchester Cathedral. This is the only picture of Cnut which is known to have been drawn in his lifetime.*

E *This is from the* Knytlinga Saga*, written in the 1250s.*

Cnut was the tallest and strongest of men, and the most handsome: except that his nose was thin, long, and somewhat hooked. He was pale, blond and hairy. No man had better eyes: fine-looking and sharp-sighted.

Activities

1 a) Read source A. What impression of Cnut do you get from this source?
b) Can you think of any ways to defend Cnut's actions?

2 Look at source B. Why did Emma of Normandy play such an important role in English history in the 11th century?

3 a) Read source C. What was the bad news for England in 1018?
b) What was the good news?

4 a) Look at source D and read source E. Using only source D, describe King Cnut's appearance.
b) Compare this description with source E.
c) Which source do you think is the most reliable and why?

5 It is 1035. You are English and have just heard news of Cnut's death. Say whether you would have been pleased or sad, and why.

20 What Effects Did the Vikings Have on England?

What effect did this type of man have on England?

The Vikings raided, invaded, and traded with most parts of England for 300 years. But what effect – big or small, good or bad – did they have? This is not an easy question to answer. One of the main problems is that no one knows exactly how many Vikings came to England.

Some think the Vikings had a great impact. After all, they conquered and ruled much of north and east England for 50 years and Viking kings ruled all England for over 25 years in the 11th century. Many English peasants received new lords, and maybe new neighbours, who spoke a different language.

Thousands of English places have names that end in 'by', 'thorpe' or 'thwaite' which are names of Viking origin. This suggests that many Vikings settled in England.

But a large number of Viking place-names does not prove that there were large numbers of Vikings. A few thousand Vikings might have conquered the north and east of England in the same way that 10,000 Normans conquered the whole of England after 1066.

Some historians think that Viking settlers brought about major changes in laws, customs and way of life. They think that by the 11th century there were great differences between the Viking north and the non-Viking south of England.

But other historians think that the differences between north and south existed before the Vikings came. Many Vikings do seem to have quickly settled down and accepted English ways, including Christianity, rather than forcing their ways on the English.

Perhaps the Vikings had a good effect on some areas. They opened up more land for farming and encouraged trade. Some new towns were founded and some old ones prospered.

But the Vikings also had a bad effect. They killed, enslaved and terrorised many people. Towns and villages were burned and looted. Many churches and monasteries were destroyed along with their precious libraries.

How many Vikings settled in England?

A *Extracts from the* Anglo-Saxon Chronicle.

865. A great Viking army came to England and took winter quarters in East Anglia.
876. The Viking leader Halfdan shared out the lands of Northumbria, and they were engaged in ploughing and making a living for themselves.
877. The Vikings moved into Mercia, and some of it they shared out amongst themselves.
892. 250 Viking ships sailed to Kent ... Then soon after this Haestan came with another 80 ships into the mouth of the Thames.

B *A map showing Viking place-names in England.*

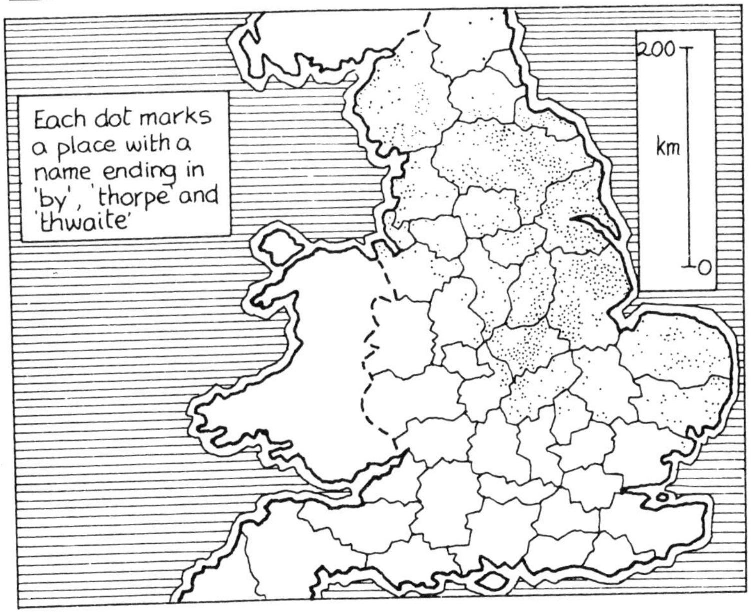

C *Patrick Wormald, a historian, wrote this in 1982.*

It has been suggested that Kings Aelle of the Northumbrians and Edmund of the East Angles were sacrificed by Ivar the Boneless to Woden in a particularly nasty way; the 'blood-eagle' involved ripping a victim's lungs out of his rib-cage and draping them across his shoulders like an eagle's folded wings ... If there is anything in these stories ... it would explain why Vikings struck such terror into Christians.

D *Simeon, a monk, wrote this in the 12th century.*

The Viking army raided here and there and filled every place with bloodshed and sorrow. Far and wide it destroyed the churches and monasteries with fire and sword. When it departed from a place it left nothing standing but roofless walls. So great was the destruction that at the present day one can scarcely see anything left of these places, nor any sign of their former greatness.

E *Magnus Magnusson, the* Mastermind *presenter, wrote this in 1980. Mr Magnusson was born in Iceland and is descended from the Vikings.*

The Vikings brought to the British Isles vigorous new art forms and vigorous new settlers; they founded and developed great market towns, they introduced new forms of administration and justice that have left their mark to this day ... They introduced the very word law into the English language!

F *Patrick Wormald, a historian, wrote this in 1982.*

Modern views of the Vikings tend to play down the size and **ferocity** of Viking attacks ... It is argued that chroniclers were always likely to exaggerate numbers and the extent of any disaster ...

The results of the Viking invasions for the English Church and English culture look serious, but the Vikings were not **fanatical** pagans, out to kill priests and destroy churches for the sake of it, but raiders looking for loot . . . and Church and learning were already in decline.

Activities

1 a) Read source A. What does this tell us about Viking settlement in England?
b) If each ship held 25 people, how many Vikings came to England in 892 AD?

2 a) Look at source B. Use an atlas and make a list of ten places that end in 'by' or 'thorpe'.
b) Does this source prove that many Vikings settled in England?

3 a) Read sources C and D. What impression of the Vikings do you get from these sources?
b) Which source do you think is the most reliable? Explain your answer.

4 a) Read sources E and F. What impression of the Vikings do you get from these sources?
b) Why might Magnus Magnusson be sympathetic to the Vikings?

5 Prepare for a class discussion. Decide whether you think the Vikings had (a) a great or small and (b) a good or bad effect on England. Write down your main arguments.

21 Harald Hardrada and the Battle of Stamford Bridge

In 1066 Edward the Confessor died. He left no children and it was not clear who should become the next English king. Harold, Earl of Wessex and the most powerful man in England, was crowned king on 6 January 1066. He had no real **blood-claim**, but said that Edward the Confessor had left him the throne.

Most Englishmen accepted Harold as king. But two men did not accept Harold. William, Duke of Normandy, believed that he had a better claim and said that both Edward and Harold had promised him the throne.

Harald Hardrada, King of Norway, said that he should be king. Viking kings had ruled England from 1016-1042. Other Vikings had a better claim than Harald but he was more ambitious and stronger than anyone else.

Strangely enough the three men claiming the English throne in 1066 were all of Viking descent. Harald was pure Viking. Harold had a Viking mother. Duke William was descended from Vikings who had settled in Normandy.

Harald, like William, set about raising an invasion force. He won the support of Tostig, Harold's younger brother. Tostig had been Earl of Northumbria. A rebellion against him in 1065 had led to his being banished from England. Tostig was angry that Harold had not helped him.

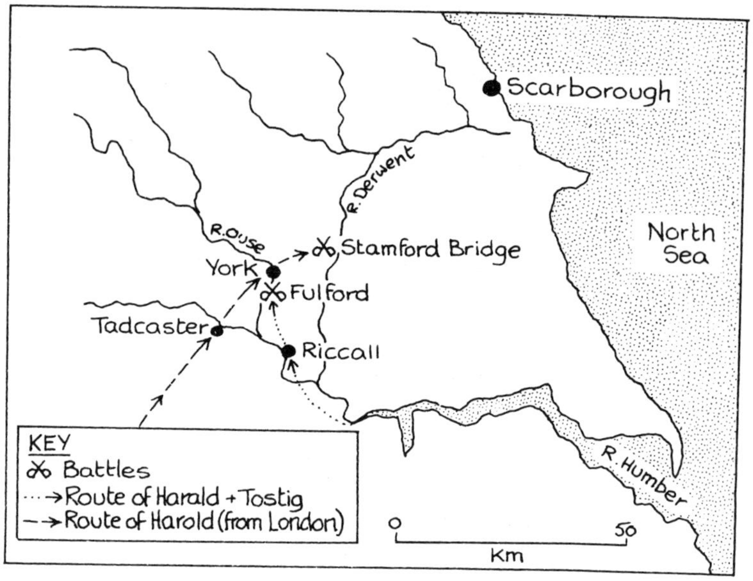

Yorkshire in 1066.

In September 1066 Harald and Tostig invaded England. They had over 300 ships and about 9,000 men. They sailed up the Rivers Humber and Ouse to Riccall and then marched on York.

On 20 September Harald defeated an English army led by Earls Edwin of Mercia and Morcar of Northumbria at Fulford. York now surrendered and gave hostages to Harald.

As soon as he heard news of the Viking invasion, Harold left London and hurried northwards with his army, gathering men on the way. On 25 September the English army made a surprise attack on the Vikings at Stamford Bridge. Harald's army was destroyed and both he and Tostig were killed.

Three days later Duke William invaded England. Harold returned south but the English army was weakened by its losses at Fulford and Stamford Bridge. On 14 October 1066 Harold was defeated and killed at the Battle of Hastings and Duke William of Normandy became King of England.

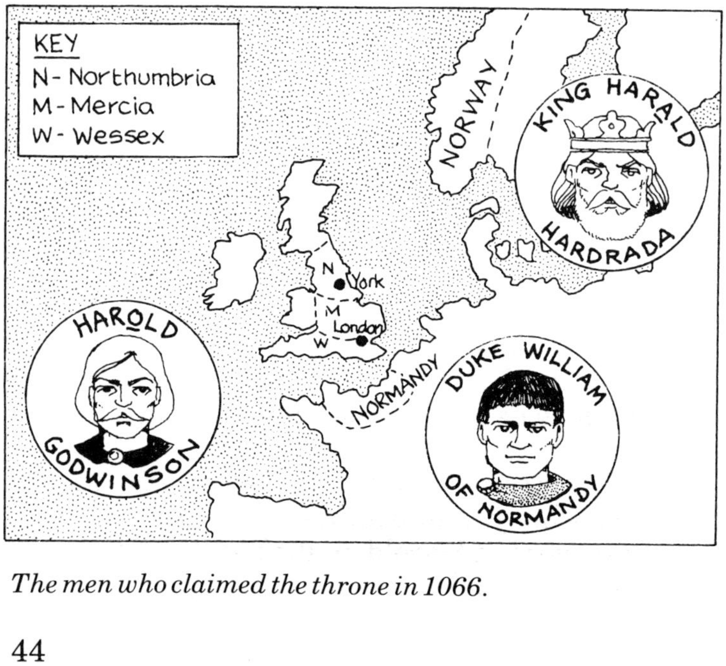

The men who claimed the throne in 1066.

A *Pictures from the Bayeux Tapestry showing soldiers fighting at the Battle of Hastings.*

B *This is from* King Harald's Saga, *written in Iceland in the 13th century.*

King Harald surpassed all men in **shrewdness** and resourcefulness . . . He was an outstandingly brave warrior, and he also had great victory-luck . . . He was a handsome man of great presence. He was fair-haired, with a fair beard and long moustaches . . . He was well over six feet tall. He was brutal to his enemies and dealt ruthlessly with any opposition to him . . . He was very greedy for power and wealth. But he was very generous to his friends.

C *An extract from the* Anglo-Saxon Chronicle.

1066. Then Harold our King came unexpectedly upon the Norwegians and met them beyond York at Stamford Bridge with a great host of Englishmen, and that day a very stubborn battle was fought by both sides. There were slain Harald Hardrada and Earl Tostig and the remaining Norwegians were put to flight, while the English fiercely attacked their rear until some of them reached their ships . . . there were few survivors, and the English had possession of the place of slaughter. The King then gave quarter to Olaf, the son of the King of the Norwegians, to their bishop, to the Earls of Orkney, and to all those who were left aboard their ships . . . and the King let them sail home with 24 ships.

D *A further extract from* King Harald's Saga.

Harald now fell into such a fury that he rushed forward ahead of his troops, fighting two-handed. Neither helmets nor coats of mail could withstand him. It looked then as though the English were on the point of being routed . . . But now King Harald was struck in the throat by an arrow, and this was his death wound. He fell, and with him fell all those who had advanced with him . . . Before the battle continued, King Harold offered quarter to his brother Tostig and all the surviving Norwegians. But the Norwegians shouted back with one voice that every one of them would rather die than surrender.

Activities

1 Write down the following paragraph and fill in the missing words.

In 1066 King ________ the Confessor died. Three men – Harold, Earl of ________, William, Duke of ________, and Harald Hardrada, King of ________, claimed the English throne. Harold was crowned king. William and Harald prepared to invade. Harald allied with ________, Harold's brother, and invaded England.

2 Read source B. Harald Hardrada did not have a very good claim to the English throne. What clues does this source give for why he invaded England in 1066?

3 a) Look at source A. What was the main difference between the way the Normans and English fought?
b) Does this picture provide any evidence about the Battle of Stamford Bridge, fought a few days earlier? Explain your answer.

4 Read sources C and D. The Battle of Stamford Bridge has just ended. Write down the message that Harold might have sent to London, giving news of his victory.

22 The End of the Viking Age

The death of Harald Hardrada at Stamford Bridge was not quite the end of the Viking Age in England. In 1069 a Danish fleet, led by sons of King Swein, sailed into the River Humber and supported an English revolt against William and the Normans. William marched north and devastated Yorkshire but he could do little against the Viking fleet.

In 1070 King Swein himself came to England. But he soon reached an agreement with William and left with much treasure. In 1085 the King of Denmark again planned to invade but in the end his fleet never set sail.

After this the Vikings did not seriously threaten England again. They were also on the decline in Scotland. By the 13th century Scottish kings had won control of northern Scotland and the Western Isles. The Orkneys and Shetland Islands remained Norwegian until the 15th century, but then they too were taken over by Scotland.

By the end of the 11th century, Viking expansion everywhere was over. Viking traders no longer travelled across Russia to the Caspian and Black Seas. Vinland and even Greenland were forgotten.

There are several reasons why Scandinavians stopped going a-Viking. One reason was that states in western Europe grew stronger and were much more difficult to attack.

Another reason was that the kings of Sweden, Norway and Denmark brought under control the great nobles who had once led Viking raids.

In the 10th and 11th centuries the kings of Denmark and Norway were converted to Christianity. These kings destroyed heathen temples and punished those Vikings who refused to become Christian. Christian Vikings were less likely to go a-Viking than heathen Vikings.

By 1100 the Viking Age, which had lasted for nearly 300 years, was over.

The Vikings' reputation.

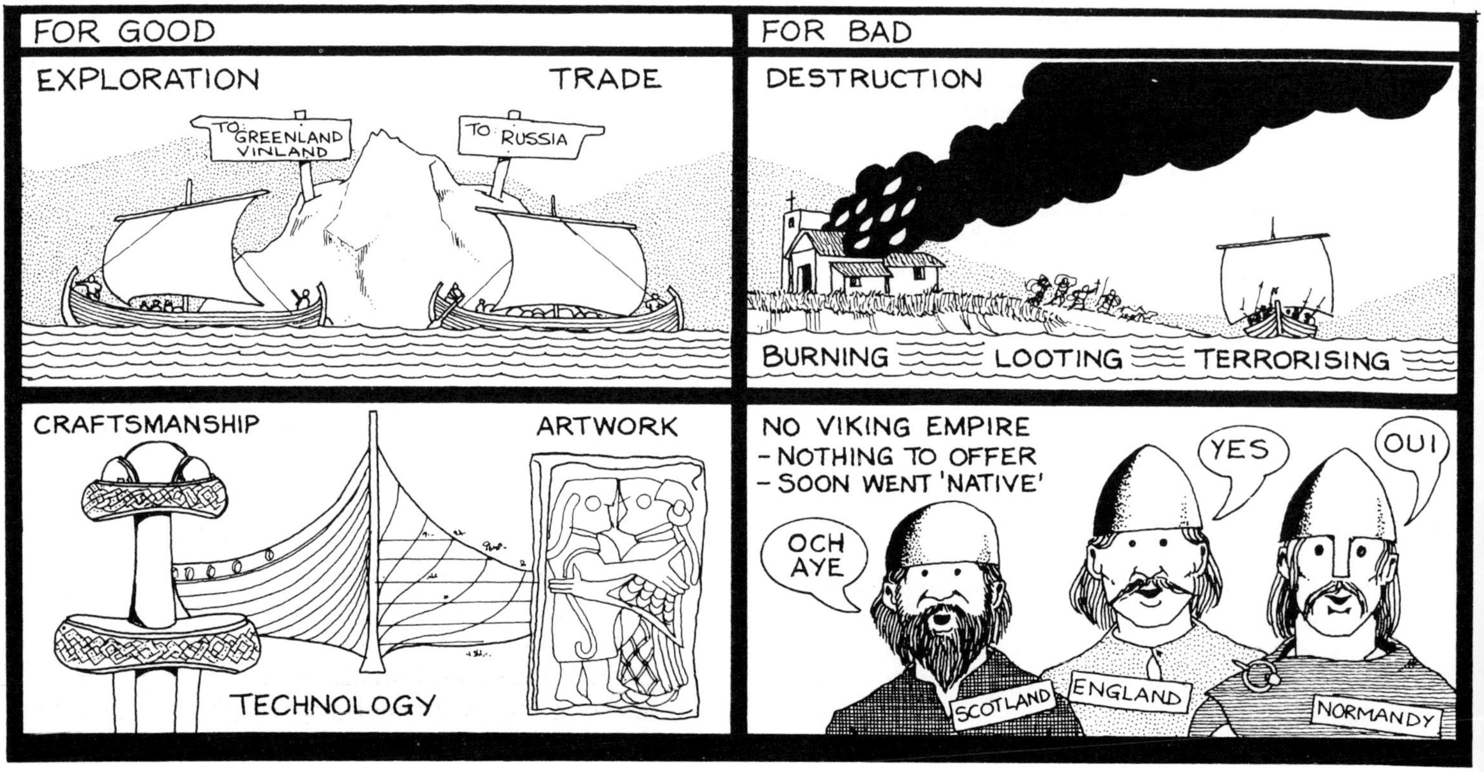

A *A map showing Viking settlement.*

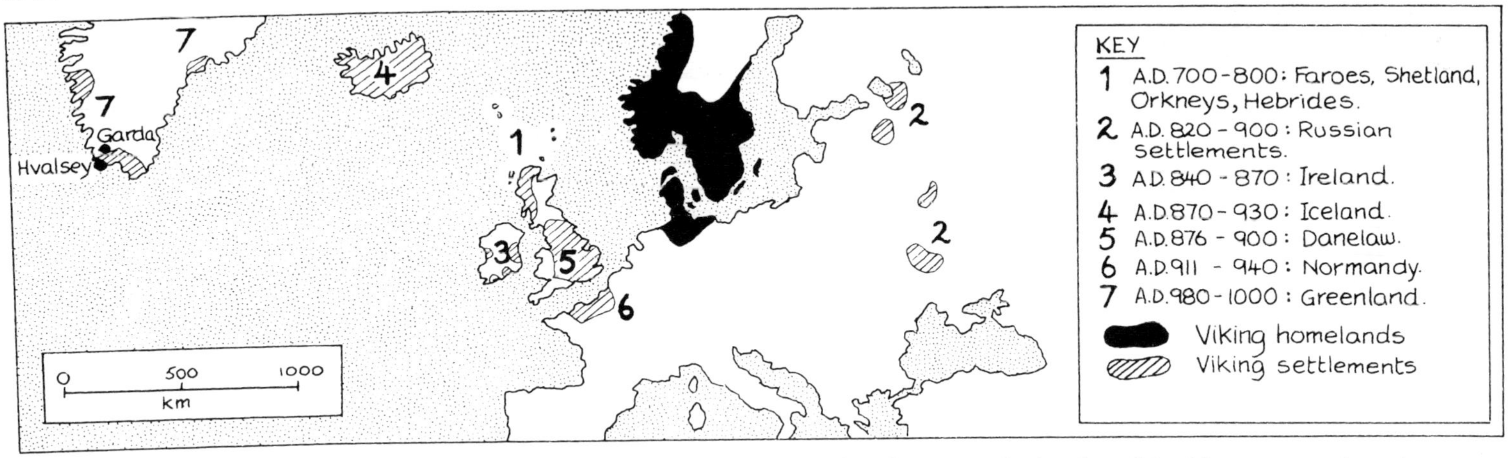

B *The* Orkneyinga Saga *tells how the Vikings in the Orkneys became Christians. King Olaf of Norway met Earl Sigurd of the Orkneys. Olaf had five warships and his men outnumbered Sigurd's.*

Olaf spoke to him in this way. 'It is my will that you and all your people are baptised. If you are not you shall die on the spot and I shall carry fire and flame through all your Isles.' Faced with this choice, Earl Sigurd decided to become Christian. Olaf had him baptised, and took as a hostage his son . . . Then all the Orkneys became Christian.

C *An extract from R R Sellman's book,* The Vikings *(1957).*

The last mention of Icelandic – or any – contact with Greenland comes in 1410. There is some reason, from 15th-century fashions found in the graves, to think that one or two ships may have arrived later than this . . .

The 15th-century descendants of the tough comrades of Erik the Red were wracked by starvation and the diseases brought with it. Their men had an average height of five feet three inches, and their women of four feet six inches. Of those discovered, few had lived to more than 30 . . .

Diseased and half-starved, without iron weapons, the people of the outlying farms gradually fell victims to the raids and surprise attacks of the Eskimo. Finally about 1500 the last Greenlander died.

D *Magnus Magnusson wrote this in 1980.*

There are Eskimo stories about the last Norseman in Greenland. They speak of an attack by the Skraelings [Eskimos] on the last surviving community, on Hvalsey. The Norsemen, it is said, took refuge in Hvalsey Church, but that night the Skraelings set fire to the church. Everyone inside was burned to death except the leader of the Norsemen, a heroic warrior called Olaf, who managed to escape through a window with his young son in his arms. The Skraelings pursued him; and after a desperate chase during which he had to abandon his son, they caught up with him at Garda. And there in the shadow of the great red sandstone cathedral, they did him to death by **sorcery**. In Hvalsey Church there is evidence to show that once upon a time it was burnt.

Activities

1 a) Read source B. Do you think this is a good way to convert people to another faith? Give reasons for your answer.
b) Why do you think there were fewer Viking raids after the Vikings became Christian?

2 Read source C. You have been sent to Greenland in the 16th century to find out what has happened to the Viking settlers. Write a report giving your conclusions.

3 a) Read source D. What evidence is there to support this story?
b) The Eskimos could not write. Does this make the story more or less likely to have happened and why?

4 Work in groups. Look at source A and think about what you have learned about the Vikings. What kind of a reputation have the Vikings left behind them? Did they have a good or bad effect on the world? Choose someone to explain your group's thinking to the other groups.

Glossary

atrocities – unpleasant, brutal, violent acts
banished – forced to leave a country
berserkers – fierce, madly-brave Viking warriors
blood-claim – to have a claim to something because you are of the same family
byrnie – a mail-shirt, worn for protection
Byzantine Empire – a great empire in Turkey and eastern Europe. The Byzantine emperors were very rich and powerful in the Viking Age. Their capital was Constantinople
caribou – a type of reindeer
civilised – at an advanced stage of development
Danegeld – a tax raised by King Ethelred to pay the Vikings
Danelaw – the area of eastern and northern England which was ruled by the Vikings in the late 9th and early 10th centuries
enslaved – made into a slave
excavation – digging up things from the past
fanatical – filled with mistaken enthusiasm for something, especially religion
ferocity – acting fiercely and cruelly
fortified – guarded and well-defended
heathen – a person who is not Christian, Jewish or Muslim
helmsman – a man who steers a ship
housecarl – the bodyguard of a Viking chief
knorr – a Viking cargo or trading ship
malt – barley or other grain used to make beer
navigational instruments – things used by sailors to help them find their way (such as a compass)
ornaments – things used in churches for purposes of worship – books, altars and so on. Church ornaments were often very valuable
overlord – someone who has power over someone else
pagans – people who worship several gods
peat – boggy soil which can be cut into pieces for fuel or building
pilgrimage – a journey to a place for religious reasons
prosperity – wealth and riches
ransom – money demanded by a kidnapper to free a hostage
replica – a copy of something
sagas – stories of Viking heroes. Most were written in Iceland in the 12th and 13th centuries
Scandinavians – people from Denmark, Norway and Sweden
shrewdness – wise, cunning, clever
slaughter – kill, massacre
sorcery – magic, witchcraft
tapestries – large pieces of cloth on which pictures or patterns have been woven or sewn
terrorised – frightened and threatened
treaty – an agreement made between kings or countries
unleavened bread – bread that has not risen; more like biscuit than bread
Valhalla – a kind of heaven for Viking warriors
Varangian Guard – regiment of Viking soldiers who fought for the Byzantine Emperor

Index